# Language in use

INTERMEDIATE

## Classroom Bo[ok]

ADRIAN DOFF & CHRISTOPHER J[ONES]



CAMBRIDGE
UNIVERSITY PRESS

PUBLISHED BY THE PRESS SYNDICATE OF THE UNIVERSITY OF CAMBRIDGE
The Pitt Building, Trumpington Street, Cambridge, United Kingdom

CAMBRIDGE UNIVERSITY PRESS
The Edinburgh Building, Cambridge CB2 2RU, UK
40 West 20th Street, New York, NY 10011–4211, USA
477 Williamstown Road, Port Melbourne, VIC 3207, Australia
Ruiz de Alarcón 13, 28014 Madrid, Spain
Dock House, The Waterfront, Cape Town 8001, South Africa

http://www.cambridge.org



First published 1994
Sixth printing 2002

Printed in the United Kingdom at the University Press, Cambridge

ISBN 0 521 43552 8 Classroom Book
ISBN 0 521 43555 2 Self-study Workbook
ISBN 0 521 43554 4 Self-study Workbook with Answer Key
ISBN 0 521 43553 6 Teacher's Book
ISBN 0 521 43560 9 Class Cassette Set
ISBN 0 521 43561 7 Self-study Cassette Set

*Split editions:*
ISBN 0 521 43559 5 Classroom Book B
ISBN 0 521 43558 7 Classroom Book A
ISBN 0 521 43556 0 Self-study Workbook A with Answer Key
ISBN 0 521 43557 9 Self-study Workbook B with Answer Key
ISBN 0 521 43562 5 Self-study Cassette A
ISBN 0 521 43563 3 Self-study Cassette B

# Contents


| | | |
|---|---|---|
| | *Guide to units* | page 6 |
| **Unit 13** | Comparing and evaluating | 60 |
| **Unit 14** | The media | 64 |
| **Unit 15** | Recent events | 68 |
| **Unit 16** | Teaching and learning | 72 |
| **Unit 17** | Narration | 76 |
| **Unit 18** | Breaking the law | 80 |
| | **Review • Conversational English** | 84 |
| **Unit 19** | Up to now | 86 |
| **Unit 20** | In your lifetime | 90 |
| **Unit 21** | Finding out | 94 |
| **Unit 22** | Speaking personally | 98 |
| **Unit 23** | The unreal past | 102 |
| **Unit 24** | Life on Earth | 106 |
| | **Review • Conversational English** | 110 |
| | *Additional material* | 118 |
| | *Tapescripts* | 125 |
| | *Reference section* | 136 |
| | *Acknowledgements* | 144 |


This book contains the second half of the complete edition of *Language in Use* Intermediate Classroom Book. Please note that page numbering from the complete edition has been retained throughout.

# Guide to units

| Classroom Book | Self-study Workbook |
|---|---|
| **13 Comparing and evaluating** | |
| Comparing things; comparing the way people do things; criticising and complaining<br>**Grammar:** comparative adjectives and adverbs; (not) as ... as ...; too & enough | Grammar exercises<br>**Listening:** *Living in Britain*<br>**Pronunciation:** *Linking words: consonant + consonant*<br>**Reading:** *Left-handedness* |
| **14 The media** | |
| **Vocabulary:** newspapers and magazines, and their contents; types of TV programme<br>**Reading and listening activity:** *Easy listening* | Vocabulary exercises<br>**Listening:** *Media habits*<br>**Phrasal verbs:** *Double meanings*<br>**Writing skills:** *Similarities* |
| **15 Recent events** | |
| Announcing news; giving and asking about details; talking about recent activities<br>**Grammar:** Present perfect simple active & passive; Past simple; Present perfect continuous | Grammar exercises<br>**Listening:** *What has happened?*<br>**Pronunciation:** *Changing stress*<br>**Reading:** *Personal letters* |
| **16 Teaching and learning** | |
| **Vocabulary:** learning things at school; skills and abilities; education systems<br>**Reading and listening activity:** *Improve your memory* | Vocabulary exercises<br>**Listening:** *Three school subjects*<br>**Phrasal verbs:** *Prepositional verbs (1)*<br>**Writing skills:** *Letter writing* |
| **17 Narration** | |
| Flashbacks in narration; changes in the past; reported speech and thought<br>**Grammar:** Past perfect tense; reported speech structures | Grammar exercises<br>**Listening:** *Locked in!*<br>**Pronunciation:** *Linking words with /w/ or /j/*<br>**Reading:** *Strange – but true?* |
| **18 Breaking the law** | |
| **Vocabulary:** types of crime; types of punishment; courts and trials<br>**Reading and listening activity:** *Detective Shadow* | Vocabulary exercises<br>**Listening:** *A case of fraud*<br>**Phrasal verbs:** *Prepositional verbs (2)*<br>**Writing skills:** *Defining and non-defining relative clauses* |
| **Review** Units 13–18 | |
| **Conversational English** | |
| 1 *Giving advice*<br>2 *Making choices* | |

## Classroom Book | Self-study Workbook

### 19 Up to now

Saying when things started; saying how long things have (or haven't) been going on

**Grammar:** Present perfect simple/continuous + for/since; negative duration structures

Grammar exercises
**Listening:** *Favourite things*
**Pronunciation:** *Stress and suffixes*
**Reading:** *Four logic puzzles*

### 20 In your lifetime

**Vocabulary:** birth, marriage and death; age groups; age and the law

**Reading and listening activity:** *A Good Boy, Griffith*

Vocabulary exercises
**Listening:** *Birth and marriage*
**Phrasal verbs:** *Three-word verbs (1)*
**Writing skills:** *Joining ideas: showing what's coming next*

### 21 Finding out

Asking for information; reporting questions; checking

**Grammar:** information questions; indirect questions; reported questions; question tags

Grammar exercises
**Listening:** *Phone conversation*
**Pronunciation:** *Changing tones*
**Reading:** *A bit of luck*

### 22 Speaking personally

**Vocabulary:** ways of describing feelings; positive & negative reactions

**Reading and listening activity:** *What's in a smile*

Vocabulary exercises
**Listening:** *James Bond films*
**Phrasal verbs:** *Three-word verbs (2)*
**Writing skills:** *Sequence: unexpected events*

### 23 The unreal past

Imagining what would have happened in different circumstances; expressing regret

**Grammar:** would have done; 2nd and 3rd conditionals; I wish + Past perfect; should(n't) have done

Grammar exercises
**Listening:** *A better place*
**Pronunciation:** *Common suffixes*
**Reading:** *If things had been different ...*

### 24 Life on Earth

**Vocabulary:** environmental problems and solutions; endangered species

**Reading and listening activity:** *The Doomsday Asteroid*

Vocabulary exercises
**Listening:** *How green are you?*
**Phrasal verbs:** *Review*
**Writing skills:** *Organising ideas*

### Review Units 19–24

### Conversational English

*1 Making offers*
*2 In the street*

# 13 Comparing and evaluating

## 1 National differences

Comparison structures

1 You will hear people from France, Japan and the USA talking about differences between Britain and their own country.
What do you think their opinions will be? Complete the sentences.

............... is much more crowded than Britain.

Britain's a safer place to live than ............... .

In Britain, people have much more respect for the law than in ............... .

In ..............., people are more interested in each other than they are in Britain.

The British don't spend as much time over their meals as the ............... .

People aren't as honest in Britain as they are in ............... .

Now listen to the recording and see if you were right. Do they mention any other differences?

2 Write down three differences between your own country and another country.

## 2 Who does it best?

Adjectives & adverbs

Amanda

I'm a faster swimmer than Brian, but he's better at singing than I am. His English isn't as fluent as mine, and you should see his handwriting – I write much more neatly!

Brian

Poor Claire – she can hardly sing at all, and she doesn't swim very fast either – not as fast as I do, anyway! But she speaks English more fluently than I do.

Claire

I wish I could sing as beautifully as Amanda – unfortunately I've got a very bad singing voice. But I speak English better than she does, and I certainly write more neatly!

| | *swimming* | *singing* | *English* | *writing* |
|---|---|---|---|---|
| Amanda | | | | |
| Brian | | | | |
| Claire | | | | |

1 **Which of these three people**
- is the fastest swimmer?
- is the best at singing?
- speaks English the most fluently?
- has the neatest handwriting?

2 **Work in threes.**
**Talk about the same activities. Find out who does each of them best.**

## 3 Not good enough

too & enough

He spoke too fast.

There wasn't enough food.

The music was much too loud.

There wasn't enough for the children to do.

It was quite interesting, but it went on far too long.

It wasn't warm enough to sit on the beach.

Too many people were smoking.

The room wasn't big enough.

1 **Look at the complaints in the bubbles. Which pictures do you think they go with?**

**What else do you think was wrong?**

2 **Continue these remarks with a complaint using** *too* **or** *enough*.

*a* My first English lesson was a disaster …
*b* I'll never go to that restaurant again …
*c* If you carry on like this, you're going to have a heart attack …
*d* Working conditions at the factory are terrible …

## 4 Awards

1 Who or what would you nominate for these awards? Think of one or two candidates for each.

2 Work in groups. Choose one of the awards, and together decide which candidate should win it.

Tell the rest of the class which candidate you chose, and why.

### Grammar Checklist

#### Comparative adjectives & adverbs

**Adjectives:** bigger, easier; **more** interesting, **more** careful.
**Adverbs:** faster, louder; **more** easily, **more** carefully.
**Irregular:** good → **better**; well → **better**.

#### Comparative structures

**... -er than**
**more ... than**

Your room is | tidier / **more** attractive | **than** mine.

She drives | faster / **more** slowly | **than** I do.

**as ... as ...**

He's **as** tall **as** his father.
I'm nearly **as** old **as** you.
My room **isn't as** tidy **as** yours.
I **don't** drive **as** fast **as** she does.

#### Big & small differences

Your room is **far/much** tidier than mine.
My room isn't **nearly** as tidy as yours.

She drives **slightly/a bit** faster than I do.
I don't drive **quite** as fast as she does.

#### too & not enough

**too** + *adjective or adverb*
**too much/many** + *noun*

You work **too** hard.
It's **too** cold to swim.
There are **too many** people here.

**not** + *adjective or adverb* + **enough**
**not enough** + *noun*

The table **isn't** big **enough**.
He could**n't** walk fast **enough**.
There is**n't enough** food to eat.

*See also Reference section, page 136.*

# Focus on Form

## 1 Big and small differences

| ... | slightly<br>a bit | *Adj.* + -er | than ... |
|---|---|---|---|
| | much<br>far | more + *Adj.* | |

*Student A:* **Can you guess the answers to the questions below? Do you think there's a big difference or a small one? Use the structures in the table.**

*Student B:* **Look at the facts on page 118. Tell A if he/she is right or wrong.**

**Example:** *Which is bigger, the Atlantic or the Pacific?*

The Pacific is much bigger than the Atlantic.

*a* Which country uses more nuclear power, France or Spain?
*b* Who lived longer, Elvis Presley or Mozart?
*c* Which is more fattening, flour or sugar?
*d* Which is bigger, Los Angeles or San Francisco?
*e* Who drink more alcohol, the British or the French?
*f* Which is higher, Mount Fuji or Mount Kilimanjaro?

## 2 Not as ... as ...

**Write sentences with** *not as ... as ...* **based on the facts in Exercise 1.**

**Example:**

The Atlantic isn't (nearly) as big as the Pacific.

## 3 Adverbs

**Look at these adjectives. Write the adverb forms in the table.**

| | *Adverb* | *Comparative adverb* |
|---|---|---|
| quick | quickly | |
| fast | fast | |
| slow | | |
| hard | | |
| early | | |
| clear | | |
| good | | |

**Use three comparative adverb forms in sentences of your own.**

## 4 Finding fault: too & enough

**What might be wrong with the things below? Complain about them using** *too* **and** *not enough.*

**Example:** *a plate of hamburgers and chips*

The chips aren't hot enough.
The hamburgers are too greasy.
There aren't enough chips.
There's too much ketchup.

*a* a cup of coffee
*b* the local bus service
*c* a bar
*d* your car
*e* your neighbours

## 5 Too/enough to ...

*Student A:* **Start a sentence using** *too* **or** *not enough.*

*Student B:* **Complete the sentence using** *to* **+** *infinitive.*

**Example:**

*A* The wall isn't high enough ...
*B* ... to keep burglars out.

| *A* | *B* |
|---|---|
| The wall isn't very high. | She doesn't go out on her own. |
| I don't play very well. | I can't go on holiday this year. |
| The water's cold. | It won't keep burglars out. |
| She speaks fast. | Children shouldn't play in it. |
| She's rather busy. | I can't understand her. |
| I haven't got much money. | Don't swim in it. |
| That road's dangerous. | She can't talk to you just now. |
| My mother's very old. | I won't get in the team. |

## 6 Pronunciation

**How do you say the words and phrases below?**

*a* Japan's much safer than the USA.
France is a bit bigger than Britain.
*b* She doesn't play as well as I do.
*c* It's not fast enough.
There aren't enough people.
*d* The wall's too high to jump over.

**Now listen and check your answers.**

# 14 The media

## 1 In print

1 Look at the picture. What are the people reading?

2 Work in groups. Answer the questionnaire.
How much have you got in common?

### *Questionnaire*

***1*** Which of your national newspapers do you think is
- the best?
- the worst?

***2*** Which of these is true?
*a* I buy a newspaper every day
*b* I buy one sometimes.
*c* I read someone else's.

***3*** Which part of the newspaper do you turn to first?
Which parts do you *never* read?

***4*** Do you buy
- a weekly magazine?
- a monthly magazine?
What do you like about them?

***5*** You're in a dentist's waiting room, and these are the only magazines on the table. Which of them would you read?

**ON OTHER PAGES**

| | |
|---|---|
| Home news | 2–5 |
| International news | 6–10 |
| Financial news | 11–12 |
| Leading articles | 13 |
| Letters | 14 |
| Arts & Entertainment | 15–16 |
| Obituaries | 17 |
| Classified advertisements | 17 |
| Horoscope | 18 |
| Cartoons | 18 |
| TV and Radio | 19–20 |
| Sport | 21–24 |
| Weather | 24 |
| Crossword | 24 |

Now imagine that your group is going on a long train journey. You can only afford *one* newspaper and *one* magazine. Can you agree on what to buy?

## 2 Changing channels

1 You will hear someone changing TV channels. Match what you hear with the programmes in the box.

| |
|---|
| cartoon<br>chat show<br>comedy show<br>crime series<br>documentary<br>game show<br>news broadcast<br>soap<br>sports programme |

Now listen again, and imagine what the person can see on the screen.

2 Which of the programmes would you carry on watching? Does your partner agree with your choice?

## 3 On the line

**Leave Us Alone, Say Royal Family**

**SOAP STAR'S SUICIDE: 'I BLAME THE PRESS' SAYS GIRLFRIEND**

**TEENAGER KILLS 5 AFTER WATCHING VIOLENT TV FILMS**

***LOVE SCENE CUT FROM TV PLAY***

***EXCLUSIVE!***

**SECRET TOXIC WASTE DUMPS: THEY *DO* EXIST**

*We reveal the truth behind the lies*

**SECRET SERVICE DOCUMENTARY BANNED**
**Not in the national interest, says Minister**

1 Look at these newspaper headlines. What do you think the stories are behind the headlines?

2 How free do you think the media should be? Mark your position on the line. What do you think the media should/shouldn't be allowed to do?

**The Press and TV should be allowed to do whatever they like.** ——— **There should be very strict controls on the Press and TV.**

Find someone whose position on the line is different from yours. Compare your opinions.

## 4 Easy listening

Reading and listening activity

***What do trains, frogs, Abba, counting sheep, motorbikes and a mother's heartbeat all have in common?***

HOW about tuning your radio to an all-day Swiss yodelling channel or settling down to an evening of uninterrupted Buddhist chanting?

From the 440 radio channels available on Osaka Yusen Broadcasting, Japan's largest cable-radio network, subscribers can tune into a channel featuring 24 hours of croaking frogs, or one that consists of the sound of trains pulling in and out of stations.

As well as the sounds of cicadas or percolating coffee, Osaka Yusen offers nearly 100 channels of announcer-free jazz, rock, classical music, Second World War military marches, and folk music from all over the world. Sheena Easton, Abba and Lionel Richie each have entire channels to themselves, although the repetition rate must be almost as high as that of an in-flight music channel. One student says that he most often listens to the channel that plays the sound of a revving motorcycle engine.

For those in search of more intellectual background sounds for their dinner parties, there is always the abacus-lesson channel or a range of talks on spiritual development. But anyone tired of all the above should adjust their sets to 'drowsing channels' and tune into the sheep-counting station, for example, which features a mature male voice slowly counting from one to a thousand. Then he starts again. In the background, there is the faint sound of a train moving slowly along a railway track.

For busy executives wishing to calm down after an awful day at work, there is a channel of slow synthesiser music, and another carrying only the sound of a mother's heartbeat. According to the company: 'Babies listen to this noise before they are born. It's a natural relaxant.'

## READING

1 What is the answer to the question above the text on page 66?

2 Which of these sentences about the text are true, and which are false?

*a* You can only listen to the radio channels at certain times of the day.
*b* On the music channels, the music is introduced by disc jockeys.
*c* 'Drowsing channels' are intended to help you get to sleep.
*d* The heartbeat channel is for babies only.
*e* There are nearly 100 channels available altogether.

3 What are these sounds like?

– *yodelling*
– Buddhist *chanting*
– *croaking* frogs
– *percolating* coffee
– a *revving* motorcycle engine

4 Look at the list on the right. Why do you think people would want to tune in to these channels?

C2 C17 H29 J32

5 Choose three channels from the list that you think you would enjoy.

## LISTENING

You will hear two foreigners who live in Japan talking about cable radio channels they listen to. The recording is in four short parts.

1 What channels do they mention? What do they use them for? Complete the table.

| | *Channels* | *What do they use them for?* |
|---|---|---|
| *Part 1* | | |
| *Part 2* | | |
| *Part 3* | | |
| *Part 4* | | |

2 Which of these words were used in each part? How did each speaker use them?

alarm clock, background music, phone box
atmosphere, meeting, pop star

Now listen again and check your answers.

**Tropical**
**C1** Sea, Waves, Seashore
**C2** Sea, Waves, Seashore + Music

**Japanese Sounds**
**C3** Waterwheel, Waterfall
**C4** Waterwheel, Waterfall + Music

**Seasonal Music**
**C5** New Year's Tunes
**C6** Music for the The Dolls' Festival and The Boys' Festival
**C7** Hawaiian, Christmas

**Background Music**
**C17** Morning Music with Birdcalls
**C18** Midnight Music
**C19** Social Dance Music
**C20** Sound of Steam Locomotives

**Karaoke**
**C23** Duets
**C24** Popular
**C25** Lessons in Karaoke

**Music for Places of Business**
**G28** Office (Slow)
**G29** Office (Up-tempo)
**G30** Bank (Slow)
**G31** Bank (Moderate)
**G32** Bank (Up-tempo)

**For Children**
**H23** Japanese and Foreign Legends
**H24** Songs from TV Cartoons
**H26** Nursery Rhymes and Songs
**H27** Music for Babies
**H28** Bedtime Stories
**H29** Lullabies
**H30** Mother's Heartbeat

**Spiritual Music**
**H31** Self-realization
**H32** Cultivating Innate Ability
**H33** Concentration (Enhancing Creativity)
**H34** Spiritual Stability (Enhancing Patience)
**H35** Easing Stress

**Drowsing**
**H36** Drowsing
**H37** Philosophical Talks
**H38** Counting Sheep

**Sounds of Nature**
**J21** Rural Scenery (Cows, Insects ...)
**J22** Rain, Wind, Thunder
**J23** Port Town (Ships, Sea ...)
**J24** Summer Scenery (Cicadas, Frogs ...)
**J25** Rooster Calls and Bells Ringing

**Ceremonial Music**
**J26** Birthday Song
**J27** Japanese Wedding
**J29** Hymns

**For Alibis**
**J30** Pachinko & Mah-jong
**J31** Telephone Booth
**J32** Bar, Coffee Shop

**Fun Corner**
**J33** Jokes & Music
**J34** Scary Music
**J35** Movie Information
**J37** Mental Exercise
**J38** Travel Information

# 15 Recent events

## 1 In the news

Present perfect • Past simple

1 These pictures all accompany news stories. What do you think has happened in each case?

Now listen to the news stories. For each story answer the questions.

- What events are reported using the Present perfect tense?
- What other details are given?

2 Think of something that's been in the news this week. Summarise the story in two or three sentences.

## 2 Tell me more

Questions

1 Look at this piece of news. What other details might you want to know? Write some questions.

Now look at the letter on page 121.
Did the writer answer your questions?

2 *a* On a piece of paper, write a sentence giving a piece of news about yourself or someone you know. Exchange sentences with your partner.

*b* Look at your partner's sentence, and write some questions asking for more details. Then give the paper back.

*c* Expand your sentence into a paragraph, adding the details your partner asked for.

## 3 What have you been doing?

Present perfect continuous & simple

Well, this month I've been serving customers as one of the staff is ill. I've also been doing the accounts, writing letters, ordering new stock. And I've bought a new delivery van.

Basically, I've been learning my lines. I suppose I've learnt about half of them now. I play an American, so I've also been taking lessons in American English.

I've been doing all the usual things – driving around, visiting clients, giving out free samples. One thing I haven't done yet is fill in this month's expenses claim. I must do that.

1 *a* Read these texts. What do you think the people's jobs are?

*b* What is the difference between the Present perfect simple (*I've done*) and the Present perfect continuous (*I've been doing*)?

2 Work in pairs. Find out whether your partner has been doing any of these things recently.

| | |
|---|---|
| – going out a lot | – spending a lot of money |
| – working hard | – watching TV a lot |
| – going to bed late | – travelling a lot |

Example:

*A* Have you been going out a lot recently?
*B* Yes, I have. I've been out four times this week.
No, I haven't. I've been painting my flat.
No. I only went out once last week.

# 4 Eavesdropping

Present perfect continuous

1 You will overhear a couple having an argument. Which of these sentences do you think are true?

*a* The woman hasn't been sleeping well.
*b* The man has found a job.
*c* The woman hasn't been working very hard.
*d* The man has been sitting around doing nothing.
*e* They haven't been getting on well for some time.

2 You will overhear bits of three more conversations. What are the conversations about? Imagine what the people have (or haven't) been doing.

## Grammar Checklist

### Present perfect active & passive

*Active:* **have/has** + *past participle*

A prisoner **has** escaped.
They **haven't found** him yet.
**Have** you **heard** the news?

*Passive:* **have/has** + **been** + *past participle*

A new planet **has been** discovered.
He **hasn't been** arrested yet.
**Have** you **been** invited to the party?

### Present perfect & Past simple tenses

**Present perfect** – *for announcing news of recent events (without saying when).*
**Past simple** – *for giving details.*

Five prisoners **have escaped** from Bedford Prison. They **broke** out late last night and **drove** away in a green van.

– **I've bought** a new coat.
– Really? How much **did** it cost?

### Present perfect continuous & simple tenses

**Present perfect continuous** – *for talking about recent activities (how you have been spending your time).*

**have/has** + **been** + **-ing**

**I've been** going out a lot recently.
She's **been** preparing for her exams.
They **haven't been** speaking to each other.

**Present perfect simple** – *for talking about single complete events.*

**I've been** tidying my room. *(An activity)*
**I've** tidied my room. (= *I've finished it.*)

**I've been** going to the cinema a lot recently.
**I've** seen three films this week.

*See also Reference section, page 137.*

# Focus on Form

## 1 Present perfect or past?

**Fill the gaps with the correct form of the verbs in the box. Choose between the Present perfect simple and the Past simple.**

| be | go | see |
|---|---|---|
| decide | make | show |
| find | offer | tell |

*a* Actress Lana Bernstein and her fourth husband ............. to separate after only two months of marriage. They ............. reporters yesterday that they both needed more time to follow their own careers.

*b* Great news! Nina ............. a job at last. She ............. for an interview last week, and they ............. her the job straight away. It's only four days a week, but the pay's good. And we ............. someone to look after the children, too.

*c* I've been having a great time since I came to Barcelona. I ............. lots of new friends, and I ............. out almost every night. Some friends of mine ............. me round the town too, so I ............. most of the sights already.

## 2 Present perfect active & passive

**Example:**

*Last week's news*   *This week's news*

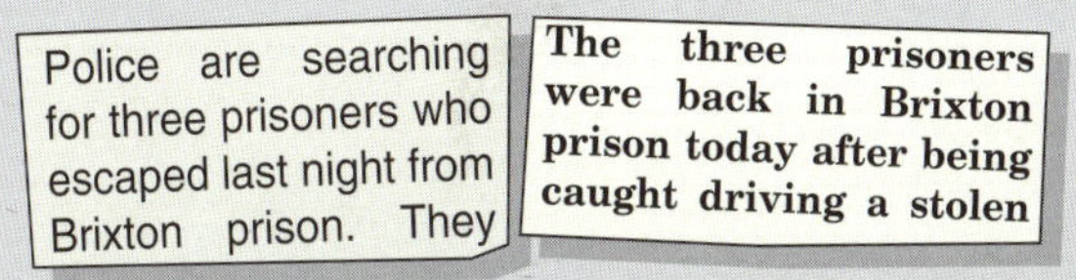
Police are searching for three prisoners who escaped last night from Brixton prison. They

The three prisoners were back in Brixton prison today after being caught driving a stolen

*A* What's happened to those prisoners who escaped last week?
*B* They've been caught.

*Student A:* **Look at last week's news on page 119, and ask B what's happened.**

*Student B:* **Look at today's news on page 120, and answer A's questions.**

## 3 Present perfect continuous

**Look at the pictures. What do you think the people have (or haven't) been doing?**

**Example:** *Picture A*

He's been watching the late movie.
He hasn't been sleeping well.
He's been working very hard.

## 4 Recent activities & actions

1 **What have these people been doing?**
2 **Add one more thing that each person has done (or hasn't done yet).**

**Example:** *I've planted some vegetables and I've cut the grass.*

1 She's been working in the garden.
2 She hasn't watered the flowers yet.

*a* We've done some jigsaw puzzles and painted some pictures, but we haven't been to the playground yet.
*b* I've washed the vegetables and put the meat in the oven.
*c* I've bought some paper hats, but I haven't ordered the cake yet.
*d* We haven't seen Buckingham Palace yet, but we have been to all the big museums.
*e* I've paid the electricity bill and the rent.

## 5 Pronunciation

**How do you say the words and phrases below?**

*a* 've we've you've they've
We've had a baby.
We had a baby yesterday.

*b* The money has been found.
The thieves have been arrested.

*c* Have you been working?
What have you been doing?
I've been watching TV.

**Now listen and check your answers.**

# 16 Teaching and learning

## 1 In the classroom

**Morden Park Secondary Sc**

Class: ............ Name: ..............

| | Monday | Tuesday | We |
|---|---|---|---|
| 9.00 | ENGLISH | | |
| 9.45 | GEOGRAPHY | | |
| 10.30 | B R | E A | K |
| 10.45 | COMPUTER | | |
| 11.30 | STUDIES | | |
| 12.15 | L U | N C | H |
| 1.30 | | | |
| 2.15 | | | |

1 *a* Look at the timetable. What other subjects would you expect to find on it?

*b* You will hear four people talking about subjects they were taught at school.
What subject are they talking about? How do you know?

2 Work in groups. Choose a subject that you all studied (or are studying) at school. Think about these questions:

- Did you enjoy it?
- What was the teacher like?
- What did you have to do?
- What *didn't* you do?
- Did you learn anything useful?

## 2 How to …

1 Do you know how to do any of the things in the box? Complete the table. Add one other thing you know how to do.

| | |
|---|---|
| windsurf | touch-type |
| bake bread | ride a horse |
| ski | shear a sheep |
| juggle | dance a waltz |
| read music | draw a bicycle |

| | |
|---|---|
| I don't know how to … | |
| I know how to … (but I'm not very good) | |
| I'm quite good at … | |
| I'm very good at … | |

2 Choose one skill you would like to know more about. What would you like to know?

Now find someone who knows more about it than you, and find out as much as you can.

Did you find out what you wanted to know?

## 3 Going through the system

You will hear someone answering questions about the American education system.

1 Look at the questions in the box. Which questions does he answer?

> *a* At what age do children start primary school?
> *b* What about secondary school?
> *c* Are all subjects compulsory?
> *d* Do all students follow the same course?
> *e* What's the school leaving age?
> *f* What are the most important school exams?
> *g* How many subjects do they take?
> *h* How long does it take to get a university degree?

2 *Student A:* Imagine you're an American. Ask about the education system in B's country.

*Student B:* Answer A's questions.

# 4 Improve your memory

Reading and listening activity

## How many days?

In some cultures, people have no problem remembering which months have 31 days and which have 30. In Iran, for example, the first six months have 31 days, the next five have 30, and the last has 28 or 29. And in Thailand, you can tell from the names of the months: those with 31 days end in *-om* (e.g. January is *Magarakom*), those with 30 days end in *-on* (e.g. September is *Kanyayon*) and February ends in *-an: Kumpapan*.

Most countries, however, use some kind of mnemonic, or memory aid. In Britain, a rhyme is used:

*30 days have September*
*April, June and November.*
*All the rest have 31*
*Excepting February alone*
*Which has but 28 days clear*
*And 29 in each leap year.*

What about your country?

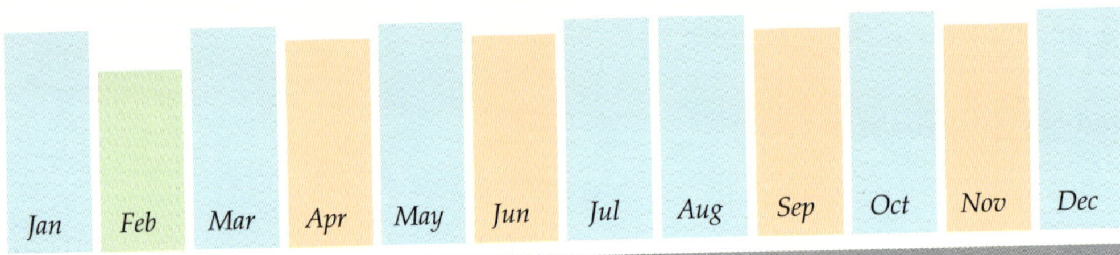


## READING

1 Look at the text called *How many days?*

How do you remember which months have 31 days and which have 30?

2 Look at the text on the opposite page, and read about *one* of the two memory techniques.

Then use the technique you have learned to test yourself.

## LISTENING

You will hear someone describing a technique for learning new vocabulary in a foreign language.

1 How does the technique use
- the learner's mother tongue?
- a visual image?

2 Look at the four pictures. For each one, note down
- the foreign word
- its meaning in English
- the 'help words' the speaker uses.

3 Choose one of the words from the two lists on the opposite page. How could you use this technique to help you learn it?

# Remembering Things in the Right Order

**Suppose you want to remember a sequence of ten unrelated items in a particular order. Here are two techniques that you can use.**

## Technique 1: Pegwords

First, you have to learn a set of pegwords, one for each of the numbers one to ten. Since each of these rhymes with its number, this is a fairly easy task. Try it for yourself:

| | | |
|---|---|---|
| One = *bun* | Five = *hive* | Eight = *gate* |
| Two = *shoe* | Six = *sticks* | Nine = *wine* |
| Three = *tree* | Seven = *heaven* | Ten = *hen* |
| Four = *door* | | |

Having mastered this, you are ready to go; suppose the ten words you are trying to remember are: *battleship, octopus, chair, sheep, castle, rug, grass, beach, milkmaid, binoculars*.

Take the first pegword, which is *bun* (rhyming with *one*), and imagine a picture of a bun interacting in some way with a battleship: you might for example imagine a battleship sailing into an enormous floating bun. Now take the second pegword, *shoe*, and imagine it interacting with *octopus*, perhaps a large shoe with an octopus sitting in it. Pegword nine is *wine*, and the ninth item is *milkmaid*, so you might imagine a milkmaid milking a cow and getting wine rather than

milk. And so on. Having created these pictures, you should be able to come up with an accurate list of the ten words in the right order.

## Technique 2: Places

First of all, think of ten locations in your home, choosing them so that the sequence of moving from one to the other is an obvious one – for example, front door to entrance hall, to kitchen, to bedroom, and so on.

Check that you can imagine moving through your ten locations in the same order without difficulty.

Now think of ten items and imagine them in those locations. If the first item is *grass*, you might imagine opening your front door and wiping your feet on a doormat made of grass. If the second is a *cabbage*, you might imagine your hall blocked by an enormous cabbage. If item number three is *sheep*, you could imagine someone in the kitchen trying to put a whole sheep into the oven. And so on.

The locations need not, of course, be in your own home. They could be a typical trip along your high street or around your place of work or school.

### Test yourself

Now try to create similarly memorable images for the ten items in either of these lists.

Then cover up the page, and see if you can write down the ten items in order.

If you haven't yet had time to learn the ten pegwords or locations by heart, write them down and use them to help you.

| | | | | | |
|---|---|---|---|---|---|
| 1 | shirt | 5 | camera | 8 | handkerchief |
| 2 | eagle | 6 | mushroom | 9 | sausage |
| 3 | paper clip | 7 | crocodile | 10 | king |
| 4 | rose | | | | |

| | | | | | |
|---|---|---|---|---|---|
| 1 | horse | 5 | watch | 8 | typewriter |
| 2 | bullet | 6 | window | 9 | jacket |
| 3 | table | 7 | ostrich | 10 | cloud |
| 4 | cigar | | | | |

Adapted from *Your Memory, A User's Guide* by Alan Baddeley.

# 17 Narration

## 1 Flashbacks

Past perfect tense

Sophie wandered aimlessly from room to room. The flat,

1

felt empty, too big for one person.

2

she wondered.

3

There was a heavy silence everywhere. She couldn't even put any music on.

4

She made herself a cup of coffee, and sat at the kitchen table, staring at the note with its familiar handwriting.

5 6

*c/o Ewa Gradowska, ul. Smolna 30 m 21, 00–837 Warsaw,* she read. No telephone number. She wondered who Ewa Gradowska was.

7 8

Not that it mattered, really. There would be no emergency, she was sure of that.

☐ 'Just in case there's an emergency,' he'd told her.

☐ which had once seemed so small,

☐ Had he known her for a long time? Years perhaps?

☐ Why had she let him leave so easily?

☐ Or had they only just met?

☐ He'd taken the cassette player. She'd agreed to that.

☐ He'd left his address in case she needed to get in touch.

☐ Why hadn't she asked him to wait and think again?

**1 Fit the missing parts back into the story. What do they all have in common?**

**2 Now fill the gaps in the text below with suitable flashbacks.**

At the top of the hill he stopped the car and looked down at the village where ...................... He saw the grey houses, the church, the park, the old schoolhouse where ...................... It was all exactly as he remembered it: the smoke drifting up from the paper factory; the old garage which had only one petrol pump; the hotel, with its bright yellow walls. And there, in the distance, was the farm. With a grin, he remembered the day, 20 years before, when ......................

He drove down to the hotel and went into the bar to get some lunch. He sat at the table by the window, where ...................... Where was she now, he wondered. Was she still living here? Or ......................?

## 2 Changes in the past

Past and Past perfect tenses

1 **Read the description below, and say what the guests had (or hadn't) done.**

As soon as I got home, I realised that it had been a mistake to let them use my flat.

- All the lights were on.
- The front door was open.
- There was no-one in the flat.
- There were cigarette burns in the carpet.
- There were piles of dirty dishes everywhere.
- There was no food in the fridge.
- The plants were all dead.

2 **Choose one of these remarks. Imagine what things were like and what had happened.**

*a* Clearly they were expecting some very important guests for dinner.
*b* When I saw her again, I didn't recognise her at first.
*c* After only one year in power, the government was already very unpopular.

## 3 Reporting

Reported speech and thought

1 **What did these people actually say (or think)? Fill the bubbles.**

They said they were police officers.

She said she would meet me at the airport.

After a time, she realised that someone was following her.

He told me he'd fought in the Vietnam War.

When I got to the station, I discovered that the train had already left.

The Prime Minister told reporters that he was not going to resign.

2 *a* **Think of a time recently when one of these things happened to you:**

- you realised that something was wrong
- someone told you a surprising piece of news
- you met somebody interesting.

**Write a sentence about it using *said*, *told*, *discovered* or *realised*.**

*b* **Tell your partner what happened. Include your sentence in what you say.**

## 4 The dead rabbit

You will hear a story called *The dead rabbit*. The story is in five parts. Listen to each part of the story and answer the questions.

*Part 1*
- What was the dog like?
- What had it done on previous occasions?

*Part 2*
- What did the dog bring home?
- What had it done?
- What do you think the man did next?

*Part 3*
- What hadn't the dog done?
- What do you think the man did next?

*Part 4*
- What did the man do?
- What happened the next morning?
- What do you think the neighbour said?

*Part 5*
- Why was the neighbour upset?
- What had the dog done?

### Grammar Checklist

**Past perfect tense**

*Active:* **had(n't)** + *past participle – for going back from the past to events that happened earlier.*

The house was empty – everyone **had left.**
She **hadn't** changed – she looked just the same.
He showed me photos of the places he**'d** visited.

*Passive:* **had(n't) been** + *past participle*

They pulled down the buildings that **had been** destroyed in the fire.

**Past & Past perfect tenses**

There **was** some food on the table.
They**'d left** some food on the table.
Some food **had been left** on the table.

The door **wasn't** locked.
They **hadn't** locked the door.
The door **hadn't been** locked.

**Reported speech & thought**

*Change the verb one tense further back:*

| | | |
|---|---|---|
| Present | → | Past |
| will | → | would |
| Past / Present perfect | → | Past perfect |

He told me he **was** a tourist.
(His actual words: '**I'm** a tourist.')

She said she **would** teach me Japanese.
(She said '**I'll** teach you Japanese.')

I suddenly discovered that **I'd lost** my wallet.
(I thought '**I've lost** my wallet.')

*See also Reference section, page 138.*

# Focus on Form

## 1 Which tense?

**Put the verbs in brackets into the correct form. Use the Past simple (*did*), the Past continuous (*was doing*) or the Past perfect (*had done*).**

The clock said 11.30. I (be) in the office for two hours, and the phone (not ring) once. Maybe I (be) in the wrong business.

I (put) my feet up on the desk, and (pick) up the morning paper. The New York Hurricanes (lose) again. The police (pull) two more bodies out of the river. Myra Halliday (just divorce) her sixth husband. Nothing new there. I (start) doing the crossword.

I (still do) the crossword when the door (open) and a man (come) in. He (be) tall, fairly good-looking, and in his mid-forties. He (wear) a white suit and a loud tie, and he (smoke) an expensive cigar. He (look) as if he (not sleep) for a week. I (see) him before. His picture (be) on the front page of the newspaper that I (hold) in my hand. He (be) Myra Halliday's latest ex-husband.

"Your boss in, honey?" he (ask).

"Where I come from, mister," I (say), "people knock before they open doors. And that's a No Smoking sign on the wall."

## 2 Explanations: the Past perfect

*Student A:* **Read out the sentences below.**

*Student B:* **Give a suitable explanation from the box, using the Past perfect tense.**

**Example:** *He had to go by bus ...*

... because his car had broken down.

*a* He had to go by bus ...
*b* He couldn't pay for the meal ...
*c* His parents bought him a new bike ...
*d* He was hungry ...
*e* He knew a lot about the French Revolution ...
*f* He couldn't get into the restaurant ...
*g* He had to stay in after school ...
*h* He couldn't get in touch with them ...

| |
|---|
| He didn't reserve a table. |
| He passed his exam. |
| He lost their address. |
| His car broke down. |
| He didn't have any breakfast. |
| He didn't do his homework. |
| He studied history at university. |
| He left his wallet at home. |

## 3 Reported speech

**Work in pairs. Last weekend you were both invited to a rather smart party. You each spent some time talking to two different people.**

**Turn to page 119 (*Student A*) or page 120 (*Student B*) to find out what they said to you. Then try and remember what they said, and tell your partner, using reported speech.**

**Example:** *'I'm a film actor. I've just come back from making a film in Hollywood.'*

He told me that he was a film actor, and that he'd just come back from making a film in Hollywood.

## 4 Pronunciation

**How do you say the words and phrases below?**

*a* The guests had arrived.
Everyone had enjoyed themselves.
The guests hadn't arrived.
She hadn't been abroad.

*b* There was someone in the room.
There were people everywhere.

*c* They said they were reporters.
He told me we'd met before.
She realised that she'd forgotten his name.

**Now listen and check your answers.**

# 18 Breaking the law

## 1 Crime ...

A **Customs officials found 5 kilos of heroin hidden inside the tyres of the car.**

B The two gunmen left the shop with more than £10,000 worth of watches and jewellery.

C **When he opened the door, she shot him three times in the chest. According to the pathologist's report he died instantly.**

D **She said she would publish the photos unless he gave her £5,000.**

E **A ransom of $1,500,000 dollars was demanded for the child's release.**

F Shortly after take-off, they produced guns and forced the pilot to fly to Cyprus, where the plane was given permission to land, and surrounded by armed troops.

G **When the school was reopened after the weekend, staff found that three classrooms had been completely wrecked: furniture and windows were broken, and graffiti had been sprayed on the walls.**

H He broke into the flat at 3.00 in the morning and took £3,000 from a cupboard.

1 Look at the extracts from newspapers and match them with the crimes in the box.

| | |
|---|---|
| blackmail | murder |
| burglary | robbery |
| hijacking | smuggling |
| kidnapping | vandalism |

What do you call the *people* who commit these crimes?

2 *a* Choose a crime and think of a real incident that you know of.

*b* Work in groups. Decide which of your stories is the most interesting.

*c* Tell the story you have chosen to the rest of the class.

## 2 ... and punishment

1 What punishments would you give for the offences in the box?

Do you think the person should

- pay a fine?
- be sent to prison?
- be sentenced to death?
- be punished in some other way?
- not be punished at all?

| shoplifting<br>dropping litter<br>spying for a foreign power<br>drunken driving<br>smoking marijuana<br>shooting a police officer<br>not paying income tax |
|---|

2 In groups, compare your answers.

## 3 Guilty or not guilty?

1 Read the news story. What was Mr Cook charged with?

2 *a* What arguments do you think were used in court

- by the prosecution?
- by the defence?

*b* Which of these things do you think happened at the end of the trial?

- Mr Cook was found not guilty.
- He was found guilty and had to pay a fine.
- He was found guilty and was sent to prison.

Now listen to a news broadcast about the trial. What happened?

### Passenger 'stabbed attacker on Tube with a swordstick'

**A COMMUTER** carrying a swordstick stabbed a man in the stomach after he tried to strangle him on a London Underground train, a court was told yesterday.

Mr Edward Cook drew his swordstick as he was held by the neck and his head was repeatedly struck against a door, it was said in Wood Green Crown Court.

The court heard that Mr Cook, aged 56, was returning home on the Victoria Line when two young men attacked him.

"One of them pushed him against the door of the carriage, holding him by the neck and banging him against the door. At that stage he took out his sword and used it on the person attacking him," Mr Michael Lawson, for the prosecution, told the jury.

The attacker, who smelled strongly of alcohol, was taken to hospital and treated for the wound. Mr Cook was arrested and charged with possessing an offensive weapon. He told police he carried the swordstick for self-defence while walking in Epping Forest. Mr Lawson said there was no lasting injury to the attacker.

After the incident Mr Cook was interviewed by police and explained why he used the swordstick.

Mr Cook yesterday

He said: "I did it as a last means of self-defence. It was a desperate act as my life was in danger."

The walking stick, which unscrewed to reveal a three-foot long blade and cost Mr Cook £400, was shown to the jury.

The case continues today.

## 4 Detective Shadow

Reading and listening activity

## LISTENING

**You will hear two people playing a game in which one person reads out a murder mystery and the other person tries to solve it.**

**There are three characters:**

- Uncle Cecil (the murder victim)
- Harry Fox (his nephew)
- Detective Shadow.

1 **Listen to the first part of the recording and answer the questions.**
   - What did Shadow see when he arrived?
   - What happened, according to Harry Fox?
   - What happened after Shadow arrived?

2 **How does Shadow know that Harry Fox is lying?**

   **Now listen to the solution. Were you right?**

## READING

**Here are four more crimes solved by Detective Shadow. What are the solutions?**

1 Shadow opened the door to Dr Adam Apple's office and looked around him. Dr Apple's head lay on his desk surrounded by a pool of blood. On the floor to his right lay a small handgun. There were powder burns on his right temple, indicating that he had been shot at close range. On his desk was a suicide note, and his right hand held the pen that had written it. Shadow recorded the time as 3.30 pm, and ascertained that death had occurred within the past hour. As Shadow was gathering clues, Dr Apple's wife burst into the office and screamed, "Good lord, my husband's been shot!" She ran toward him, saw the note and cried, "Why would he want to kill himself?"

"This was no suicide" said Shadow. "This was clearly a case of murder." How does he know?

2 "I have the only key to the room containing the jewellery of my late aunt Maggy," said Sid Crook. "Since her death a week ago, neither I nor anybody else has entered this room. I was quite pleased to hear all her jewellery was to be sold and the proceeds to go to charity," continued Crook.

Shadow removed a huge plant whose broad leaves were turned towards the wall, partially covering the safe. While Crook was opening the combination lock, Shadow crossed the room to sit on the ledge of the large bay window. Crook opened the safe, and removed the bag of jewels. "I'm sure these jewels will fetch a fortune for charity," said a smiling Sid Crook. "I'll bet these jewels are either fake or there are a few missing," replied Shadow. What made Shadow suspicious?

3 "Mr Grey?" inquired Shadow, "I'm afraid I have some bad news for you. Your brother-in-law is dead and I have reason to believe he was murdered."

"Oh no!" replied Grey. "I just saw Sam a couple of days ago. To tell you the truth though, I'm not surprised. Sam did have a big mouth and quite a few enemies. As a matter of fact both of my sisters' husbands and Sam had a big fight over a business deal that went wrong. Then there was a friend of my brother's who lent Sam a lot of money and never got it back. Another person is my wife's brother who just got out of jail. He accused Sam of framing him. He swore he would get even." As Grey talked on about Sam's enemies, Shadow got out the handcuffs and arrested him on suspicion of murder. Why?

4 Jim Cool waited until Ed Fry left the office of author Harry Queen. Cool slipped on a pair of gloves, took a handgun from his desk, and crossed the hall to Queen's office. As Queen looked up to see who was there, Cool took aim and shot. Cool dropped the gun on the floor, picked up the telephone on Queen's desk and called the police. He then went back across the hall to his own office and hid the gloves. Shadow arrived moments later and Cool told his story. "I was working at my desk when I heard a shot. I ran to the hall and saw a man fitting the description of Ed Fry running from Queen's office. I went to Queen's office and found him lying on the floor dead. I immediately picked up the phone on Queen's desk and called the police."

Several hours later Shadow arrested Cool for murder. Why was he so easily caught?

All five cases are adapted from *MindTrap* ©, under license to Spears Games ®.

# Review: Units 13–18

## Find out

1 *A* Which person in your family are you closest to in age? Tell B who it is.
*B* Find out how different A is from the person he/she has chosen. Ask about
– appearance – personality
– interests – abilities.

2 Find out from other students what kinds of TV programmes they enjoy and don't enjoy watching.
Who do you have most in common with?

3 In groups, talk about what you've been doing recently. Find out
– who's been enjoying themselves the most
– who's been the busiest.

## Role-play

**MILLIONAIRE FOUND MURDERED AT COUNTRY RESIDENCE**

*A* You're the housekeeper. You discovered the body this morning. What did you find? How had the victim been murdered?
*B* You're the dead man's secretary. You spent yesterday working with him. Who else was there? Did anything unusual happen?
*C* You're the police officer investigating the case. What have you found out so far? Do you suspect anyone?
*D* You're a journalist. Think of questions to ask A, B and C.
Then interview A, B and C. Report what they said to the rest of the class.

# Conversational English

## 1 Giving advice

1 Look at the pictures above. What problems do the people have? Which bubble should go with which picture?

2 What advice would you give the person below?

*My husband's father came to live with us after his wife died while he looked for somewhere else to live. This was six months ago, and he's still here. I feel sorry for him, but he's quite difficult, and he does nothing to help around the flat. I want him to go, but my husband seems to like having him around.*

Now think of a problem of your own and ask different people for some advice. What was the best (and worst) advice you received?

## Talking points

Choose one of these topics. Take it in turns to say a sentence or two about it.

**Two towns in your country. How are they different?**

**Radio stations**

**Today's news**

**'I'd like to be good at ...'**

**What's wrong with the education system**

**'Do you know the joke about ...?'**

**'When I was a child, I believed ...'**

**Smuggling**

## Words

1 What are/were
- your best three subjects at school?
- your worst three subjects at school?

2 Add words to these lists.
- foreign news, advertisements ...
- primary school, secondary school ...
- burglar, murderer ...

3 Answer these questions.
- Where would you find a *headline*?
- What happens in a *chat show*?
- Have you ever learnt anything *by heart*?
- What's the penalty in your country for *shoplifting*?
- What does a *jury* do?

# 2 Making choices

1 You will hear four short conversations in which people make choices.

*a* What is going on in each conversation?

*b* How do the speakers use the expressions in the box?

| I'll ... |
|---|
| I'd like ... |
| I'd rather ... |
| I'd prefer ... |

2 Look at these situations.
How do you think the people might use the expressions in the box?

*Situation 1*

*Student A:* Your boss B is going abroad on a business trip. You have to arrange travel and hotel accommodation. Find out what he/she wants to do.

*Student B:* Decide how and when you want to travel and what kind of hotel and hotel room you'd like.

*Situation 2*

*Student A:* You want to go to an exhibition which is only open today and tomorrow. You'd like A to come with you.

*Student B:* There's a good film on TV, and you're feeling tired. You're not busy tomorrow.

Now choose one of the situations and act out a conversation.

*Situation 3*

*A & B:* You're in a restaurant. Look at the menu and decide what to order.

STARTERS

Tomato soup
Pâté with toast and butter
Melon
Deep-fried mushrooms

MAIN COURSES

Salmon in cream sauce with seasonal vegetables
Cheeseburger with French fries and mayonnaise
Mushroom omelette with mixed salad
Chicken and prawn with black bean sauce & noodles
Lamb curry (medium hot) with boiled rice and salad

SWEETS

Fresh fruit salad
American apple pie with ice-cream
Death-by-chocolate gateau, served with cream

DRINKS

Mineral water
Fruit juice
Cola
Beer
Red wine
White wine
Coffee
Tea

# 19 Up to now

## 1 Favourite things

Present perfect + for/since

1 Read these extracts from a magazine article.

*a* Which objects is the woman describing?

*b* How long has she had each one? Complete these sentences.

– She's had it for ...
– She's had it since ...

**Favourite things**

*Novelist Jo Hamilton, 26, takes us on a guided tour of her favourite possessions*

" I bought this ______ while I was travelling in Southern Morocco about eight years ago. It's very precious to me because I had very little money at the time and I spent a whole day bargaining to get it at a good price. I used to have it on the floor, but it started to get a bit worn, so now it hangs on the wall of my living room. "

" This was always my favourite ______ when I was a child – I was given it for my third birthday, and for years I used to take it everywhere with me. These days I keep it in my bedroom, and even after all this time it's very comforting to know it's there keeping an eye on me while I'm asleep. "

" This ______ used to be my grandmother's – my grandfather gave it to her when they got engaged. She gave it to me when I got married five years ago, and asked me to pass it on to my own grandchildren, which is just what I intend to do. It's not worth very much, but I think it's beautiful, and I only wear it on very special occasions. "

2 *Student A:* Write a sentence describing one of your favourite possessions. Don't say how long you've had it or where you got it. Give your sentence to B.

*Student B:* Imagine how long A has had the thing, and why it is important to him/her. Make some notes.

Now tell A what you thought. How far were you from the truth?

## 2 Then and now

Present perfect simple & continuous • Past simple

1 **Write the missing sentences in the table.**

| | *How long ago ...?* | *How long ...?* |
|---|---|---|
| *a* | She started playing the trumpet two years ago. | She's been playing the trumpet for two years. |
| *b* | ........................................................ | I've been a member of Greenpeace for six months. |
| *c* | ........................................................ | Estonia has been independent since 1990. |
| *d* | They met in 1954. | ........................................................ |
| *e* | They came to stay with us three days ago. | ........................................................ |
| *f* | ........................................................ | He's been working here since he left school. |
| *g* | I opened this bank account when I went to college. | ........................................................ |
| *h* | Mozart died more than 200 years ago. | ........................................................ |
| *i* | ........................................................ | He's been playing professional football for 10 years. |

2 **Write three true sentences about yourself. Choose verbs from the box.**

| | | |
|---|---|---|
| start | live | be |
| play | join | meet |

## 3 It's a long time since ...

Negative duration structures

1 **You will hear three people talking about things they haven't done for a long time.**

*a* **Listen and complete the table.**

| | *Activity* | *When did they last do it?* | *Why did they stop?* |
|---|---|---|---|
| *1* | | | |
| *2* | | | |
| *3* | | | |

*b* **The speakers use three different structures to say when they last did things. What are they?**

2 **Work in groups.**

**Think of something you used to enjoy doing that you haven't done for a long time. Tell the others about it, and answer any questions they may have.**

# 4 Guess how long ...

1 'We're just celebrating our diamond wedding anniversary.'

How long have they been married?

2 *a* How long is it since the Big Bang?
*b* How old is the Earth?

*c* How long have dinosaurs been extinct?
*d* How long ago did *homo sapiens* appear?

3 What's wrong with these statements?

*a* 'My grandfather's had the same biro since 1935.'
*b* 'Shakespeare drank tea constantly while he was writing his plays.'

*c* 'I've just bought a new Citröen 2CV.'

4 How long have these countries been independent?

*a* The United States of America.
*b* India.
*c* Latvia.

5 How long ago ...

*a* ... was the Great Pyramid built?

*b* ... did the Beatles have their first No.1 hit?

*c* ... did Mao Tse-tung die?

1 Work in groups. Do you know the answers to these questions? If you don't know an answer, make a guess.

Now listen to the answers. The group with the nearest answer scores one point. Who won?

2 Now make up two more questions, and see if other groups can answer them.

## Grammar Checklist

### Present perfect continuous tense

**have/has been + -ing** – *for talking about activities that started in the past and are still going on.*

He's **been trying** to phone her for three hours. (*not* ~~he's trying~~)
They've **been going** out together since June.

### Stative verbs

**be, have** *(= possess)*, **know**
*No continuous form – use Present perfect simple.*

I've **had** these jeans for five years.
She's **been** away for nearly a month.

### for & since

I've known them **for** years.
I've known them **since** 1975.
I've known them **since** we first moved here.

### How long ...? & How long ago ...?

**How long** + *Present perfect continuous or simple*

– **How long** has she been working here?
– For three months.

– **How long** have you been in this flat?
– Since June.

**How long ago** *(or* **When***)* + *Past tense*

– **How long ago** did she start working here?
– Three months ago.

– **When** did you move into this flat?
– In June.

### Negative duration structures

I **haven't ridden** a bike since I was a child.
**It's** ages **since** I (**last**) rode a bike.
**The last time** I rode a bike was in 1982.

*See also Reference section, page 139.*

# Focus on Form

## 1 For & since

**Complete these sentences about yourself (1) using *for* (2) using *since*.**

**Example:** *I've had this watch ...*

... for six months.
... since October.
... since my last birthday.

*a* I've been in this room ...
*b* I've been learning English ...
*c* I've had these shoes ...
*d* I've had this coursebook ...
*e* I've been at this school ...

## 2 Since when?

*Student A:* **Choose one of the events in the box and imagine what things have been like since then.**

*Student B:* **Can you guess which item A was thinking of? Complete each sentence using an item from the box.**

**Examples:**

*A* He's been eating in expensive restaurants ...
*B* ... ever since he won the lottery.

*A* He's been depressed ...
*B* ... ever since his girlfriend left him.

| | |
|---|---|
| ... (ever) since | he left school.<br>he won the lottery.<br>he visited the USA.<br>his girlfriend left him.<br>he lost all his money.<br>he crashed his car.<br>he came out of hospital. |

## 3 How long ...? & How long ago ...?

**Ask your partner these questions. If the answer is 'Yes', ask a question with *How long ...?* or *How long ago ...?***

**Example:**

*A* Do you do anything to keep fit?
*B* Yes. I play basketball.
*A* How long have you been playing?
How long ago did you start playing?

Do you know anyone who comes from a different country?

Have you got a pet?

Have you got a bike/motorbike/car/boat?

Do you do anything to keep fit?

Do you play any board games?

Do you have any relatives living abroad?

## 4 Negative duration

**Add a sentence to these remarks, saying how long it is since something happened.**

**Example:** *I'm starving ...*

I haven't eaten since breakfast.
I haven't eaten for six hours.
It's six hours since I had anything to eat.

*a* I'd love to visit Berlin again ...
*b* I don't think she likes me any more ...
*c* I'm afraid my Spanish is rather rusty ...
*d* It's no good asking me what's on at the cinema ...
*e* He's the laziest person I know ...

## 5 Pronunciation

**How do you say the words and phrases below?**

*a* He's been trying to phone you.
They've been talking for hours.

*b* How long have you known him?
How long has she been waiting?
How long have they been talking?

*c* I haven't been there for years.
He hasn't been out since the weekend.

**Now listen and check your answers.**

# 20 In your lifetime

## 1 Birth, marriage and death

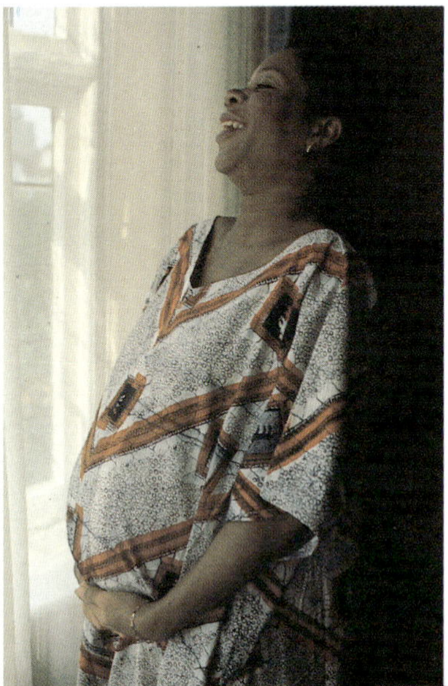

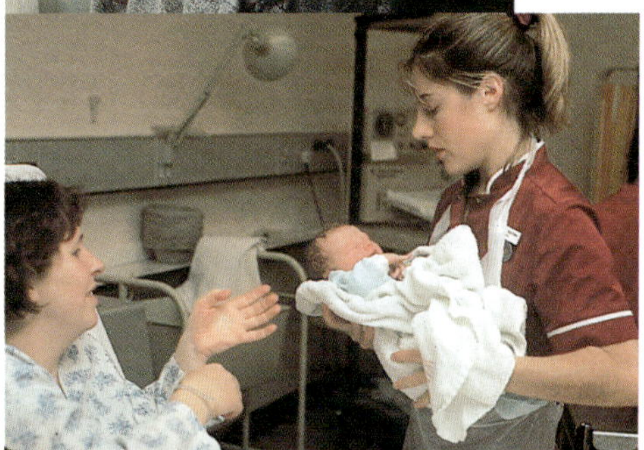

1 What vocabulary do you associate with birth, marriage and death? Write a list of words for each group of pictures.

2 You will hear five people describing birth, marriage and death customs in different parts of the world. Here are some of the things they talk about:

| | | |
|---|---|---|
| silver | money | eating and drinking |
| a white dress | sweets | dancing |
| chopsticks | flowers | songs |

Which do you expect to be about birth, which about marriage and which about death?

Now listen to the recording.

Think of birth, marriage and death customs in your own country. Which do you think a foreigner would find the most unusual?

## 2 Age groups

| Childhood |
|---|
| Adolescence |
| Young adulthood |
| Middle age |
| Old age |

1 Look at these age groups. At what age do you think you move from one to another?

2 Look at the adjectives. Do you think they apply to any particular age group?

Think of some other adjectives that could go with each age group.

**helpless** **ambitious** **rebellious**
**self-conscious** **naughty** **shy**
**wise** **lonely** **independent**

## 3 Legal age

### Age and the law: some facts about Britain

**School-leaving age**
Children have to stay at school until the age of 16. There is no upper age limit.

**Alcohol**
You have to be 18 to buy alcohol in a shop or a pub, but if you're 16 and you're having a meal in a pub, you can drink beer or wine with it.

**Prosecution**
In Scotland, you can be prosecuted for a crime at the age of 8. In England and Wales, the age is 10. You can't be sent to prison until you're 21.

**Motor vehicles**
16-year-olds can ride a motorbike of up to 50 cc. At 17 you can ride any bike or drive a car.

**Smoking**
You can smoke cigarettes at any age, but you can't go into a shop and buy them until you are 16.

**Armed forces**
Men can join the army at 16, women at 17. If you're under 18, you need your parents' consent.

**Marriage**
You can get married at 16 with your parents' consent. Otherwise you have to wait till you're 18.

**Paid employment**
You can take a part-time job at 13, and a full-time job at 16 (i.e. when you've left school).

**Voting**
Anyone aged 18 or over can vote in a general election.

**Retirement age**
Women can retire on full pension at 60. Men have to wait till they're 65.

**Entering Parliament**
The minimum age for becoming a Member of Parliament is 21. The youngest person to become an MP in the 20th century was Bernadette Devlin, who was elected a week before her 22nd birthday.

Read the text about British law.

What do *you* think should be the legal age for these activities? Fill in the table.

Compare your answers with your partner's.

| | | | |
|---|---|---|---|
| Leaving school | | Joining the army | |
| Drinking alcohol | | Getting married | |
| Being prosecuted | | Getting a job | |
| Riding a motorbike | | Voting | |
| Driving a car | | Retirement | |
| Smoking | | Entering Parliament | |

# 4 A Good Boy, Griffith

Reading and listening activity

## READING

Read each section of the story in turn and answer the questions.

*Section 1*

What can you tell about

- Griffith?
- Blodwen?
- Morgan?

*Section 2*

What else do you now know about the three characters?

*Section 3*

| Griffith gave a ring to Gwen ... | → | ... He wants to give the ring to Gwen again. |
|---|---|---|

What happened in between?

*Section 4*

What is Griffith's problem?

## DISCUSSION

What do you think will happen next? Imagine an ending to the story.

## LISTENING

You will hear the last two sections of the story.

*Section 5*

Does Griffith bring the money?
Does Blodwen give him the ring?
What does Blodwen promise?

*Section 6*

*'Blodwen felt her heart capsize.'* Why?
What does Morgan think happened?
What actually happened?

# A GOOD BOY, GRIFFITH

**by Leslie Thomas**

1 GRIFFITH came over the hill behind the pit and turned the bend in the lane to the red brick cottage. It was too early for Morgan to be home from the garage yet, he knew that. Blodwen would be alone. Walking up to the gate he noticed how the windows shone clean in the late afternoon sun. Just like her, of course; always neat and decent. Never a speck of dust, never a thing out of place. She might have been his wife, but it was a good job she wasn't. He would never have been able to keep things the way she wanted them.

2 She came to the door almost immediately.

Griffith shyly reached for his cap. 'Hello Blod,' he said. 'Hope you don't mind me ...'

'What d'you want, Griffith?' she asked suspiciously. 'It's not decent for you to be calling on me, you know. Not now I'm wed; an' people knowing how we were an' all. What d'you want?'

'Well, let me come in and I'll tell you, girl. Don't keep me out here.'

For a moment she was undecided. Then she opened the door wider and he went into the living room. 'Just as I thought,' he mused. 'Not a plate out of place. Poor old Morgan. A good man, too.'

He looked at her, wondering if this could be the same girl he had asked to marry him on the night of the Institute dance. He realised now what a narrow escape he had had.

3 'Blod,' he said determinedly. 'I've come about the ring.'

A look of slow, smug triumph settled across her face. 'I thought you might,' she said. 'What about it? If you think you're getting it back, think again.'

He paled a little. 'Look, Blod,' he pleaded, 'it's important right now. Anyway, Morgan's given you a tidy little ring. Much better that one is.'

'Who do you want it for this time?' she said craftily. 'Seems that ring's been around a bit already.'

He told her that Gwen had come back.

'You know Gwen,' he said encouragingly.

She laughed, a mean little laugh with no laughter in it. 'Oh, Griffith. You're going round in circles. She was the one before me.'

And the only one, thought Griffith. You caught me on the rebound. Now she has come back from Cardiff, and she is going to stay, and she says it was all her fault, and she wants to start again.

'But why do you want the ring, Griff? Jenkins in 4
the High Street has plenty in the window.'

Griffith lost his temper. He went red about the roots of his black hair, and he banged his fist down so that the table shook and it scared her. 'Listen, Blod,' he said. 'I want that ring. I'll pay you. She doesn't know I gave it to you. She wants the same one.'

'Then it's fifty pounds, Griffith,' she said abruptly.

He gasped: 'Fifty! Don't be daft, Blod. It's not worth ten.'

'Fifty,' she repeated firmly.

'But I haven't got that much and I couldn't get it. Talk sense, girl.'

'There's some lovely dresses in Cardiff, Griff. Saw them in the paper. Morgan's taking me down in the car on Tuesday ...'

He went out and slammed the door after him.

* * *

The next afternoon he went up the hill to the red

# 21 Finding out

## 1 Information questions

Question forms

1 Look at the answers in the bubbles. What do you think the questions were?

2 Write down three 'answers' about yourself, and show them to your partner. Can he/she guess what the questions are?

## 2 I'm not sure …

Indirect question forms

| A | B |
|---|---|
| Who is she going out with? | I wonder who she's going out with. |
| How much money do I owe you? | I can't remember how much money I owe you. |
| How long is the Amazon? | I've no idea how long the Amazon is. |
| Have you met before? | I'm not sure whether you've met before. |
| When did they arrive? | Can you tell me when they arrived? |
| Has the train left yet? | Do you know if the train's left yet? |

1 *a* **What's the difference between the sentences in Column A and those in Column B?**

*b* **Combine these sentences to make indirect questions.**

- Will they come to the party? I wonder.
- How long has he been asleep? I'm not sure.
- When does the concert begin? I don't know.
- Have I read that book? I'm not sure.
- What's 'car' in Spanish? Do you know?
- What was I looking for? I can't remember.

2 **Write some true sentences beginning:**

I wonder … I'm not sure …

I don't know … I can't remember …

## 3 Getting to know you

Reported question forms

I was in the students' room waiting for my class to begin when the girl in the next seat asked me which class I was in …

I was sitting in a corner when a guy came up and asked me if I knew anyone at the party. I said I didn't …

I was waiting for my bus yesterday when a woman came and stood next to me and asked me how long I'd been waiting …

1 *a* **Read the texts. What do you think were the actual questions?**

*b* **Now listen to the scenes, and report the other questions.**

2 **In pairs, choose one of the situations above, and improvise a short conversation.**

*Student A:* **You want to get to know B. Think of one or two questions you might ask to get a conversation going.**

*Student B:* **Respond in any way you want.**

**Now report your conversation to the class.**

## 4 Tags

**Question tags**

It's a bit cold today, …

Auckland isn't the capital of New Zealand, …

They speak Arabic in Iran, …

They didn't stay very long, …

You haven't seen my glasses, …

That film was awful, …

Penguins can't fly, …

… can they?

… don't they?

… is it?

… have you?

… isn't it?

… did they?

… wasn't it?

1 **Add the missing question tags to these remarks.**

**Now listen to the same remarks. In which ones**

– does the speaker really want to find out something?
– is the speaker just expressing an opinion or belief?

2 **What question tags might you use in these situations?**

– You've just seen someone you think you recognise.
– You're driving to the airport to go on holiday.
– Your dinner guests have just left.
– You've just seen a Charlie Chaplin film.

**Choose one of the situations and improvise a short conversation.**

## Grammar Checklist

### Wh- questions

**What kind** of coffee do you like?
**What make** is your cooker?
**What happened** to your coat?

**How long** did it take to get there?
**How much** does the suitcase weigh?

**Whose** coat is this? (*not* ~~Who's~~)

### Indirect questions

**Wh-** *word + normal word order*

I don't know **what** his name **is**.
(*not* … ~~what is his name~~)
I wonder **where** they **went**.
Can you tell me **when** he's **coming** back?

**if/whether** + *normal word order*

I can't remember **if I posted** the letter.
(*not* … ~~did I post~~ …)
Do you know **whether** Mr Smith **lives** here?

### Reported questions

**Wh-** *word or* **if/whether** + *normal word order. Verb tense changes as in reported speech. (See Unit 17.)*

'Do you know many people?' he asked.
→ He asked me **if I knew** many people.

'Where are you going?' she asked.
→ She asked him **where** he **was going**.

### Question tags

They **live** here, **don't** they?
You **phoned** him, **didn't** you?
He's very talkative, **isn't** he?
You **can** drive, **can't** you?

She **doesn't** like fish, **does** she?
They **haven't** forgotten, **have** they?

*See also Reference section, page 140.*

# Focus on Form

## 1 Questions with How ...?

| | | |
|---|---|---|
| How | How long | How much |
| How far | How many | How often |

**Fill the gaps with expressions from the box.**

*a* ......... children have you got?
*b* ......... did you get here? On foot?
*c* ......... is it from Rome to Pisa?
*d* ......... did it cost?
*e* ......... expensive was it?
*f* ......... does it take you to get to work?
*g* ......... does the ferry go? Once or twice a day?
*h* ......... have you known them?
*i* ......... sugar do you take?
*j* ......... high is Mount Everest?

**Now write three questions of your own.**

## 2 Questions with What ...?

**Make questions with *What ...?* plus an item from each box.**

| | |
|---|---|
| kind of | flavour |
| sort of | colour |
| type of | size |
| make of | |

| | |
|---|---|
| soup | music |
| flowers | crisps |
| curtains | car |
| shoes | T-shirt |

**Examples:**

What sort of shoes should I wear?
What size curtains do we need?
What colour T-shirt did you get?

## 3 Quiz: indirect questions

**Ask your partner questions beginning *Do you know ...?***

**Examples:**

*When is St Valentine's Day?*
Do you know when St Valentine's Day is?
*Are spiders insects?*
Do you know if spiders are insects?

*a* When is St Valentine's Day?
*b* Are spiders insects?
*c* How many days are there in a fortnight?
*d* Why can't you swim in the Sea of Tranquillity?
*e* What nationality was Christopher Columbus?
*f* When did he discover America?
*g* Is Denmark a monarchy?
*h* What is a *didgeridoo*?
*i* Where does Batman live?

## 4 Reported questions

Are you on a business trip?
Have you ever done this sort of work before?
Where does it hurt?
Have you been taking anything for the pain?
How long are you planning to stay?
When will you be able to start?
When did the trouble start?
Can you speak Spanish?

**Report the questions you think were asked**

*a* at a job interview
*b* at the doctor's
*c* going through customs.

**Example:**

The doctor asked me where it hurt ...

## 5 Checking: question tags

**Decide whether you think these statements are true of your partner. Check by asking question tags.**

**Example:** *You like spicy food.*

You like spicy food, don't you? *or*
You don't like spicy food, do you?

*a* You like spicy food.
*b* You were born in this country.
*c* You can say 'Thank you' in Arabic.
*d* You've had measles.
*e* You believe in ghosts.
*f* You're left-handed.
*g* You know how to ski.

## 6 Pronunciation

**How do you say the words and phrases below?**

*a* What kind of biscuits do you want?
What flavour ice-cream is that?
What colour is his shirt?

*b* I wonder what they're doing.
I'm not sure if we've met.

*c* He asked me if I spoke Japanese.

*d* You're not going, are you?
*(I really want to know.)*
You're not going, are you?
*(I'm just checking.)*

Now listen and check your answers.

# 22 Speaking personally

## 1 Feelings

1 **How might you feel in these situations? Choose the best words from the box.**

*a* You're sitting chatting to friends after a good meal.
*b* Somebody has slashed the tyres on your car.
*c* You're introducing someone to a friend and you get his name wrong.
*d* It's your sixth birthday tomorrow.
*e* Your best friend is much more popular than you are.
*f* You're about to make a speech in public for the first time.
*g* You're alone in a house at night and you hear a window being opened downstairs.
*h* You've lost your wedding ring.
*i* Your neighbour keeps coming round and asking to borrow things.
*j* All the news in the papers seems to be about wars and disasters.
*k* You've heard a rumour that the factory where you work is going to close down.

| angry<br>annoyed<br>depressed<br>embarrassed<br>excited<br>frightened<br>jealous<br>nervous<br>relaxed<br>upset<br>worried |
|---|

2 **What makes you angry? depressed? jealous? ...?**
**Choose three feelings and write down a situation for each.**

**Find out if other students would feel the same.**

## 2 Reactions

1 You will hear five short scenes. For each one, find two expressions that describe what happened.

Now listen again, and say what happened in more detail.

... tried to persuade him ...

... apologised ...

... was absolutely delighted ...

... got angry ...

... refused ...

... complained ...

... tried to cheer him up ...

... gave her ...

... was very upset ...

... tried to calm her down ...

2 Work in pairs. Choose any two of the expressions and prepare a short scene of your own.

## 3 Reviews

1 Look at the words in the box.

*a* Which of them are positive and which are negative?

*b* Which adjectives would fit in these sentences?

– It was very .......................
– It was absolutely .......................

| | |
|---|---|
| amusing | awful |
| boring | brilliant |
| disappointing | dreadful |
| dull | fascinating |
| enjoyable | terrible |
| entertaining | terrific |
| exciting | wonderful |
| interesting | |

2 *a* Look at these extracts from reviews. What do you think they're about?

It was a terrific match. Hodges is one of the most exciting players I've seen for ages.

The plot was entertaining enough, but I wish the author hadn't included all those long, boring descriptions of southern England.

**This was a complete waste of an evening. The script was awful, the acting was wooden, and the camerawork was dreadful.**

*b* Choose something that several of you have seen or read recently, and write a short review.

Now find out if other people agreed with you.

# 4 What's in a smile

Reading and listening activity

## READING

1 **Before you read:**

*a* Which of these smiles do you think are real? Which are false? How can you tell?

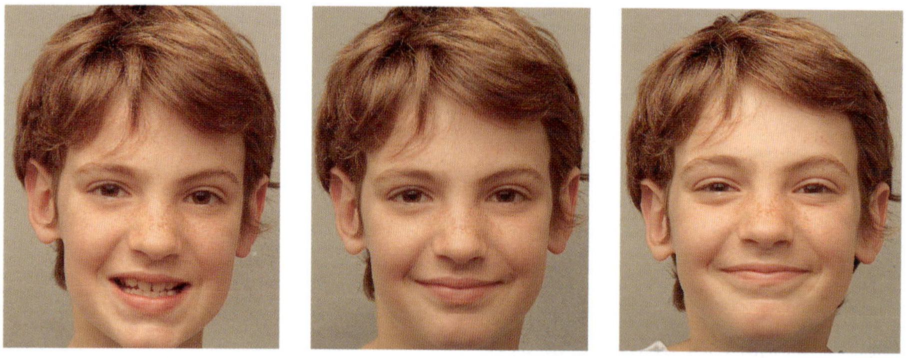

*b* Look at these faces. Which smile do you find the most attractive, and which the least attractive? Why?

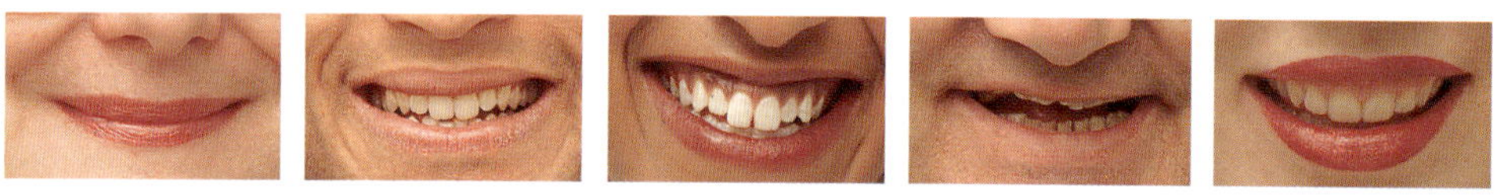

2 **Read the magazine article and find the answers to these questions.**

*a* Do people smile in every culture in the world?
*b* How many facial muscles do you use to smile?
*c* What happens to your blood pressure when you smile?
*d* What's the difference between a false smile and a real smile?
*e* How did Norman Cousins cure himself?
*f* Where can you find 'laughter rooms' and what are they for?
*g* Why did Aristotle Onassis wear dark glasses?
*h* What does a professional laugher do?

3 **Note down any points in the article that you disagree with or find hard to accept. Compare notes with your partner.**

**LAUGHTER CLINIC**

**Robert Holden, whose handbook *Laughter, The Best Medicine?* will be published early next year, runs the only NHS Laughter Clinic in Britain. Holden believes that laughter and smiling can not only heal the mind but the body as well.**

## LISTENING

1 **Read the text about the Laughter Clinic.**
**What kind of activities do you imagine take place there?**

2 **You will hear someone describing a typical session at the Clinic.**
**Make a list of all the activities she mentions.**

**Now compare your list with your partner's. Did you have the same answers?**

# What's in a *smile*

## *Smiling is …*

**universal.** In his travels, Charles Darwin discovered that smiling was the only facial expression which was recognised instantly all over the world.

**easy to see.** It is possible to recognise a smile on someone's face at a distance of 45 metres. You'd have to be much closer to decide whether the person was showing surprise, anger or fear.

**simple.** You only use one facial muscle to smile. This is the zygomatic major muscle, which reaches down from the cheekbone to the corners of the lips. To look sad or angry, you need to use at least two muscles.

**good for you.** Studies in the USA have shown that when you smile your heart rate slows down, your blood pressure goes down and the body begins to relax. This happens whether you are feeling happy or not. In fact, if you're feeling unhappy, the simple act of smiling is the first step to feeling better.

**attractive.** According to American dentists Melvin and Elaine Denholtz, an attractive smile should show most of the upper teeth, at least two thirds of the length, and just the tips of the lower teeth.

## *Real smiles and false smiles*

When you smile a real smile, two things happen to your face: your lips move up towards your cheeks, and your cheeks themselves go up and gather in the skin around the eyes. And a real smile will usually only last for up to four seconds.

False smiles are seen on the faces of politicians who have just lost an election, people who are pretending they're pleased to see you, and door-to-door salesmen. False smiles usually appear slightly too early or too late, and they tend to go on for too long.

But if you really want to know if a smile is real or false, look at the eyes. In a false smile these don't change – however much the person has practised smiling.

Eyes are important in other ways, too. When you feel good, your pupils get larger; when you feel bad, they become small. Ancient Chinese traders always looked their customers straight in the eye. If the pupils became big, the person was interested, and they could ask for more money.

### DARK GLASSES

*One reason why shipping tycoon Aristotle Onassis always wore dark glasses may have been so that his eyes would not give him away during delicate business negotiations.*

## *Laughter: the best medicine*

In 1964 an American journalist called Norman Cousins developed a serious problem with his back. It turned out that he had an illness called ankylosing spondylitis, which was extremely painful and, according to doctors, incurable. He was admitted to hospital, unable to move, and prescribed a course of strong pain-killing drugs. Cousins knew that negative emotions could make you ill, and began to wonder whether positive emotions – and particularly laughter – might make you better.

He stopped taking the drugs, and moved out of the hospital into a hotel room, which was not only a more cheerful place to be but was also much cheaper. There he hired a lot of Marx Brothers and *Candid Camera* films, and started to watch them. He found that every time he laughed, the laughter acted as an anaesthetic and gave him relief from pain. And the effect lasted some time: 10 minutes' laughter could give him around two hours free from pain.

More important, he found that he was slowly getting better, and eventually recovered completely from the illness.

For many years, the medical profession refused to take Cousins' claims seriously, but now things are changing and some American hospitals have set up 'laughter rooms', where patients can watch videos, listen to cassettes and read joke books, instead of sitting around feeling depressed.

### LAUGHING FOR MONEY

*A Frenchwoman, Julie Hette, works as a professional laugher. For a fee, she will come and laugh non-stop for you. Her record is 90 minutes. She guarantees that you will soon be laughing with her – even though you might not know what you're laughing about.*

# 23 The unreal past

## 1 Dilemmas

would have done

On 13 October 1972 a plane carrying 45 passengers and crew bound for Santiago, Chile, crashed in a remote part of the High Andes. After waiting several days, the 27 survivors of the crash realised that they had no chance of being rescued. They were stranded high in the mountains above the snow line, and although they could shelter from the worst of the cold inside the plane, they had nothing to eat except snacks and chocolates that the plane had been carrying. These soon ran out, and they were faced with starvation. Then one of the survivors suggested that there was just one chance of survival: they could eat the flesh of the passengers that had died in the crash …

1 *a* Read the story about the crash in the Andes. What was the dilemma facing the survivors?

Imagine you were one of the survivors. What would you have done?

*b* You will hear three people saying what they would have done in the situation.

Which speaker's opinion is closest to your own?

2 Work in groups. Look at one of these other dilemmas. What would you have done?

When the nine-year-old daughter of Ernest and Regina Twigg died in 1988, the post-mortem examination showed that she was not in fact their daughter. They made enquiries, and discovered that someone had made a mistake at the hospital where Mrs Twigg had had her baby girl: their daughter had been given to another couple, and the Twiggs had been given the other couple's baby. Their daughter, they learnt, was living with her 'family' in another part of the USA, 1,500 kilometres away …

In August 1991, Dr Nigel Cox was treating a 70-year-old woman who was extremely ill with rheumatoid arthritis, and in constant pain. There was no chance that she would ever leave her bed again. The only way Dr Cox could relieve her pain was by giving her large doses of heroin. After a time, however, heroin was not enough to stop the pain, and the woman begged Dr Cox to give her a drug that would kill her …

## 2 If …

Past conditionals

1 Look at the remarks above. What are the speakers talking about? What happened (or didn't happen)?

2 Write *If* … sentences based on the remarks below.

Why didn't you tell me you were ill?

Sorry. I didn't know it was your birthday.

It's a pity the weather was so bad.

It's a good thing they didn't open my suitcase.

I didn't have any money with me.

## 3 A better place

2nd & 3rd conditionals

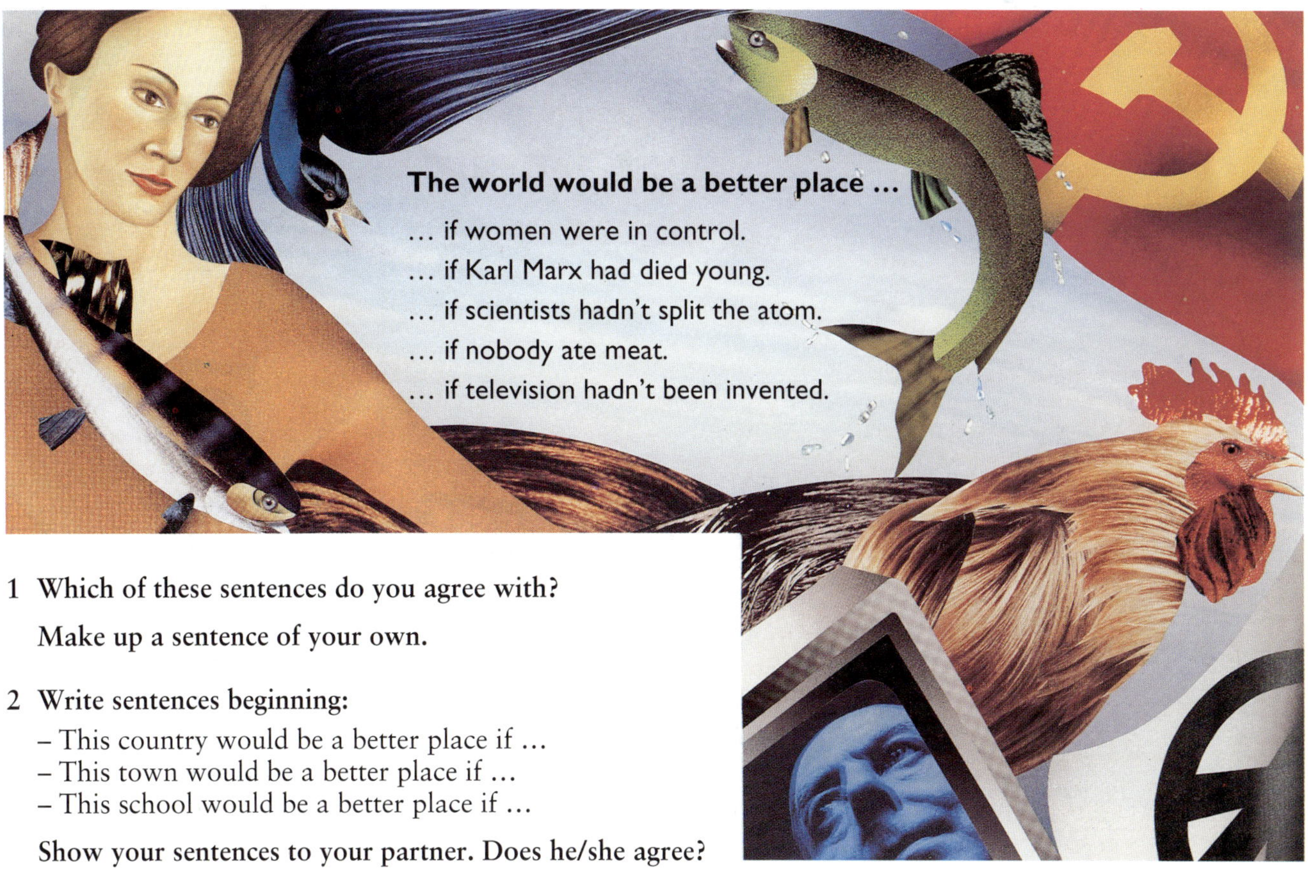


1 Which of these sentences do you agree with?

Make up a sentence of your own.

2 Write sentences beginning:

- This country would be a better place if …
- This town would be a better place if …
- This school would be a better place if …

Show your sentences to your partner. Does he/she agree?

## 4 I wish I hadn't ...

I wish + Past perfect • should(n't) have

# ‹‹‹ ARE YOU THE PERSON YOU'D LIKE TO BE? ›››

### *Analysing your regrets is the first step to finding out*

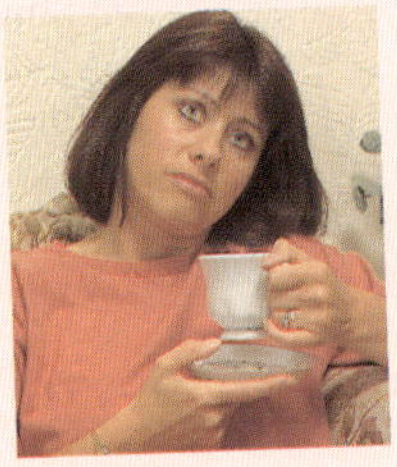

From time to time, we all find ourselves regretting things we've done and things we haven't done. But there's no point in getting depressed about it. In fact, looking at our regrets can be a very useful way of finding out more about ourselves.

***Try this test.***

**FIRST** fill in the table. Put a tick against each regret, to show whether you feel it often, sometimes or never.

**THEN** add two more regrets that you often (or sometimes) feel.

**NOW** look at the results. What do they tell you about yourself?

| *Here are ten common regrets. How often do you say them to yourself? Add two more of your own.* | *often* | *some-times* | *never* |
|---|---|---|---|
| 1 **I shouldn't have lost my temper.** | | | |
| 2 **I should have said what I really thought.** | | | |
| 3 **I wish I'd kept my mouth shut.** | | | |
| 4 **I wish I hadn't spent so much money.** | | | |
| 5 **I shouldn't have left it to the last minute.** | | | |
| 6 **I wish I'd been a bit friendlier.** | | | |
| 7 **I should have offered to help.** | | | |
| 8 **I wish I'd remembered ...** | | | |
| 9 **I shouldn't have let it upset me.** | | | |
| 10 **I should have refused.** | | | |
| 11 | | | |
| 12 | | | |

1 Look at the sentences in the table.
How do we use *I wish* and *I should* to express regret?

2 Read the article and follow the instructions.
What do your answers tell you about yourself?

## Grammar Checklist

### would have done

**would have** + *past participle – to refer to the unreal past.*

I **would have** phoned you, but I was too busy. (= actually I didn't phone you)
I **wouldn't have** enjoyed living in the 16th century.

### 3rd conditional structures

**If** + *Past perfect* ... **would have** + *past participle*

I **would have** phoned you if I **hadn't been** so busy.
If he'**d taken** a map, he **wouldn't have got** lost.
If **I'd known** they were at home, I **would have** visited them.
If she **hadn't left** the window open, the cat **wouldn't have got** in.

### 'Mixed' conditionals

*These mix 2nd and 3rd conditionals. One part of the sentence is about the past, the other is about the present.*

If he **hadn't stolen** the money, he **wouldn't be** in prison. (= he stole the money, so now he's in prison)
Inflation **would be** higher (now) if the Democrats **had won** the election (last year).

*(For 2nd conditionals, see Unit 9.)*

### Structures for expressing regret

**I wish** + *Past perfect*

I wish **I'd** apologised.
I wish I **hadn't lost** my temper.

**I should(n't) have** + *Past participle*

I **should have** apologised.
I **shouldn't have lost** my temper.

*See also Reference section, page 141.*

# Focus on Form

## 1 Would(n't) have done

**For many years, Detective Shadow has been pursuing Sid Moriarty, a master of disguise and the cleverest criminal in North America ...**

**Read the story. How many reasons can *you* find?**

**Example:**

Moriarty wouldn't have used his own sword. He would have used another weapon.

'We've got him this time, sir!' the Sergeant told Shadow excitedly. 'It was Moriarty all right!'

'Tell me about it, Sergeant,' said Shadow.

'Well, sir, for a start, the victim was killed with a 17th century Italian sword, of a kind that Moriarty is known to have in his collection.'

'How do you know?' asked Shadow.

'We found it, sir. He dropped it in the hallway. And it's got his fingerprints on the handle. Not only that, a ring with *SM* engraved on it was found by the body.'

'Mm,' said Shadow. 'Anything else?'

'Plenty! It seems the victim didn't die immediately: he had time to write *MORIA* in his own blood before he died. And we found a note in his pocket: it said *Tonight you die*, and it was signed *Sid M*.'

'Is that all?' asked Shadow, smiling.

'Not quite,' said the Sergeant. 'There's a neighbour, a Mr Sam Crook, who says he saw someone answering Moriarty's description enter the building just before midnight.'

'Right,' replied Shadow. 'You'd better arrest Sam Crook.'

'Sam Crook, sir? But ...'

'Sergeant,' said Shadow patiently, 'I can think of at least seven reasons why Sid Moriarty didn't commit this crime.'

## 2 Past conditionals

***Student A:* Read out the items from Box A. Use *If + had(n't)*.**

***Student B:* Complete each sentence with a suitable item from Box B. Use *would(n't) have*.**

**Example:**

*A* If they'd promised to lower taxes ...
*B* ... they would have won the election.

*A*
They didn't promise to lower taxes.
They didn't know you were coming.
They didn't have life-jackets.
They lit a fire.
They weren't insured.
They didn't check the plane properly.
The dog barked.

*B*
They were rescued.
They drowned.
They woke up.
They didn't find the bomb.
They ate all the food.
They didn't win the election.
They didn't get their money back.

## 3 Mixed conditionals

**Put the verbs in brackets into the right form. Use the Past or Past perfect tense.**

**Example:** *She wouldn't be so lonely ...*

... if she *knew* more people.
... if she *hadn't moved* away from home.

*a* They'd be much better off ...
... if they (not buy) such a big house.
... if they both (have) jobs.

*b* She'd still be at university ...
... if she (pass) her exams.
... if she (work) harder.

*c* He'd be much happier ...
... if he (live) in a warmer climate.
... if his wife (not leave) him.
... if he (not spend) all his savings.

**Now make some continuations of your own.**

## 4 Regrets

**Make sentences with *I wish* or *I should(n't)* for these situations.**

**Example:** *You were behind a lorry on a narrow road; you tried to overtake it; you didn't see a car coming the other way, and you crashed.*

I shouldn't have overtaken the lorry.
I wish I'd seen the car coming the other way.
I should have been more careful.
I wish I hadn't crashed.

*a* You left school at 16; you didn't go to university; now you haven't got enough qualifications to get a good job.

*b* You found a briefcase lying on the pavement; you picked it up and opened it; it exploded, and now you're in hospital.

*c* You met someone you liked; he/she wanted to marry you but you weren't sure; he/she married someone else and now you're alone.

## 5 Pronunciation

**How do you say the words and phrases below?**

*a* I would have waited.
You wouldn't have liked the film.
If I'd known you were busy, I would have waited.

*b* If he hadn't left fingerprints, they wouldn't have caught him.

*c* I should have apologised.
I shouldn't have bought it.

**Now listen and check your answers.**

# 24 Life on Earth

## 1 Global issues

1 Every week, a staggering 10,000 square kilometres of tropical rainforest are cut down. An area the size of France disappears every 12 months.

2 The nations of the world, rich and poor alike, continue to regard the sea as a convenient place to dump millions of tons of chemicals, sewage and industrial waste.

3 There are now more than 800 nuclear power stations throughout the world. Although this is supposed to be a 'clean' form of energy, there are in fact very high risks associated with it.

4 Smoke from factories and coal-fired power stations not only pollutes the air, but also causes chemical changes in the atmosphere which result in acid rain.

5 In 1985 it was noticed that there was a hole in the ozone layer over the Antarctic. Scientists now believe that the loss of ozone may be as much as 30%, and still rising.

6 Over the last 10 years, the Sahara has advanced southwards by an average of 20 kilometres per year, and 250,000 square kilometres of land has turned into desert.

7 A major report on global warming has warned that average world temperatures will rise by several degrees in the next century, due to the build-up of carbon dioxide and other 'greenhouse gases' in the Earth's atmosphere.

1 Look at the texts, and give a title to each one.
Which picture best illustrates each text? What's the connection?

2 Together, choose one of the issues. Then work in pairs.

*Pair A:* You think Pair B should be more worried about this issue. What will you say to them?

*Pair B:* You think Pair A are worrying about nothing. What will you say to them?

Now get together. Can you persuade the others to change their minds?

## 2 Going green

### FIVE THINGS YOU CAN DO TO HELP THE ENVIRONMENT

1. If it isn't very far, walk or cycle – leave the car at home.
2. Have a shower instead of a bath.
3. When you go shopping, don't ask for a bag – take one with you.
4. Don't throw away old bottles – take them to a bottle bank.
5. Don't buy furniture made from tropical hardwoods.

### FIVE THINGS GOVERNMENTS COULD DO TO HELP THE ENVIRONMENT

1. Double the price of petrol.
2. Introduce water meters.
3. Put a tax on plastic bags.
4. Put a deposit on bottles to encourage people to return them.
5. Ban the import of tropical hardwoods.

1 Which suggestions do you think are better – those for individuals or those for governments?

2 Add another pair of suggestions, one for individuals and one for governments. Ask other students which suggestion they think is better.

## 3 Endangered species

1 Work in four groups. Choose one of these animals, and make a list of all the things you know about it (or think you know). In your list, try to guess the answers to these questions.

- Where does it live?
- Why is it in danger?
- Roughly how many are there in the world?
- Is the number increasing or decreasing?

Turn to the back of the book and read about the animal. Were your guesses correct?

2 Tell other groups what you know about your animal.

Now hold a collection. Each student has $500 to spend on the animal(s) of their choice.

Which group collected the most money?

# Death of the Dinosaurs

65 MILLION YEARS AGO, dinosaurs suddenly became extinct, together with a large number of other species. But why did it happen?

Many scientists believe that the cause was a large asteroid crashing into the Earth. According to this theory, the asteroid threw huge amounts of dust and water vapour into the atmosphere, blocking out the light of the sun, the vegetation died off, and the dinosaurs starved to death.

Evidence for the theory came in 1992 when scientists in Mexico uncovered an underground crater 175 kilometres wide, which turned out to be exactly 65 million years old. The crater was probably caused by an asteroid 10 km in diameter hitting the Earth at thousands of miles an hour, with the force of 70 million one-megaton bombs.

According to David Raup of the University of Chicago, this was just one of many such cases. He says that asteroids have caused more than half of species extinctions since life on Earth began 600 million years ago. If he's right, it seems likely that *Homo sapiens* will end its days in the same way.

## READING

Find answers to these questions in the texts.

1 Look at the pictures at the top of page 109. Which shows
- an asteroid?
- a comet?

2 How did dinosaurs become extinct? What evidence is there?

3 Which asteroid has caused the most damage during the 20th century?

4 What damage would the following cause?
- an asteroid 30 metres wide
- an asteroid 1 kilometre wide
- Swift-Tuttle's comet

5 What are the chances of
- a 1 km wide asteroid hitting Earth during your lifetime?
- a 5 km wide asteroid hitting Earth next year?
- Swift-Tuttle's comet hitting Earth on August 14, 2116?

6 How is NASA planning to use
- telescopes?
- nuclear bombs?

## DISCUSSION

1 Do you think that the human race will go the same way as the dinosaurs?

2 Do you think NASA's plans are
- sensible?
- pointless?
- dangerous?

## LISTENING

1 Imagine that you read the following headline in your daily newspaper:

**10 KM ASTEROID**
**HEADING FOR EARTH**
**Due to arrive in 6 months' time**
**The chances of impact are 70%**

What would you do?

2 You will hear five people saying what they would do in the same situation.

If you had to spend the next six months with one of the speakers, which one would you choose?

### Asteroids and Comets

*Asteroids are lumps of rock flying around in space. They are fragments of planets that have broken up.*

*Comets are chunks of ice surrounded by dust. The dust is visible as a long tail trailing behind the comet.*

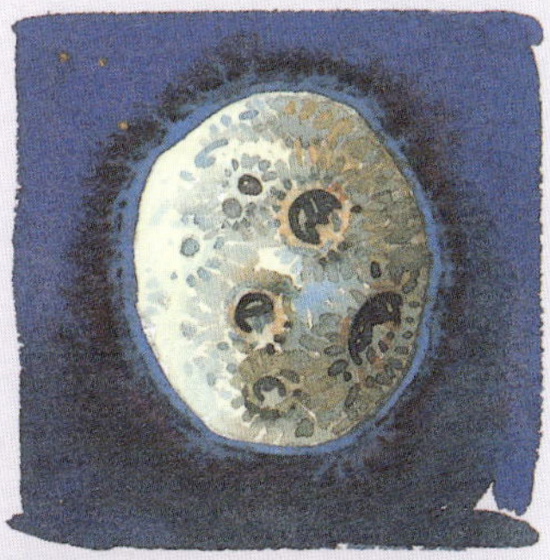

## Some recent encounters with asteroids

**1908**

A 60-metre asteroid exploded in the air about 8 kilometres above the Tunguska region of Siberia, destroying hundreds of square kilometres of forest. The explosion was equivalent to 20 hydrogen bombs.

**1978**

A huge explosion equivalent to 100,000 tons of TNT was detected in the South Pacific. This was first thought to be a secret nuclear test, but most experts now think it was an asteroid strike.

**1991**

An asteroid 10 metres in diameter passed between the Earth and the Moon, scoring a near miss.

**1992**

An asteroid called Toutatis, measuring 3 km across, passed within 3 million km of Earth. Toutatis is a regular visitor, and in 2004 it is expected to come even closer, within 1.5 million km of Earth.

| Size | How often? | Damage |
|---|---|---|
| 10 m–100 m | every 300 years | Most explode on hitting the Earth's atmosphere, and cause no damage. Some of the larger ones, however, get through, including two this century. If either of these had arrived over a major city, millions of people would have been killed. |
| 1 km | every 300,000 years | An asteroid this size could affect whole countries, with tens of millions of deaths in a densely populated region. The impact would throw up enough debris into the atmosphere to block out the light of the sun for several years. |
| 5 km | every million years | This would be big enough to cause mass extinction. Agriculture and civilisation would certainly be destroyed, and the human race might not survive. |

*The bigger they are, the harder they fall: some vital statistics about asteroids*

## NASA to the rescue

As we can't predict when a really big asteroid will arrive, is there really any point in worrying about it? NASA thinks there is. It estimates that there are between 1,000 and 4,000 asteroids at least 1 kilometre in diameter which regularly cross Earth's orbit. If such an asteroid hits the Earth once every 300,000 years, this gives the average person roughly a one in 4,000 chance of being around when it happens. A small risk, maybe, but much bigger than the risk of dying in an air crash, which is one in 20,000.

NASA aims to set up six new telescopes and spend the next 25 years working out which large asteroids are likely to arrive within the next century or two.

The idea is that once they've identified an asteroid heading straight for us, they can move it out of the way by hitting it with powerful nuclear bombs. One expert recently proposed inventing a new nuclear bomb, 10,000 times as powerful as anything we have at the moment. He did not explain how.

## August 14, 2116 – the End of the World?

**Dateline 26 October 1992**

WHILE SOME BELIEVE man-made pollution or a nuclear war may bring civilisation to a close, the end of the world is more likely to come in the shape of a huge chunk of ice and dust called Swift-Tuttle's comet, an Australian Conference was told yesterday.

New research indicates that its probable date of impact with Earth is August 14, 2116, said David Steel of the Anglo-Australian Observatory. It is not known if the collision will come in the morning or afternoon.

The size of Swift-Tuttle, which is travelling at 200,000 kph, is calculated at between five and 10 kilometres wide. The chance of collision is calculated at one in 400. Scientists

Adapted from *New Scientist*, *The Times*.

# Review: Units 19–24

## Find out

1 Find out what hobbies other students have got, and how long they've been doing them.

2 Find out about a time recently when your partner felt one of the following:

| | | |
|---|---|---|
| – angry | – embarrassed | – nervous |
| – frightened | – worried | – jealous |

3 Work in groups. Find out how 'green' other students are. How do they try to help the environment? What do they do that's bad for the environment? Who's the 'greenest' person in the group?

4 In groups, choose a TV programme that you all watched recently. What did you think of it?

## Role-play

1 Choose one of these situations, and improvise a conversation:
– A is interviewing B for a job.
– A is a police officer who has just stopped B for driving too fast.
– A is going through customs. B is a customs officer.

Now report your conversation.

2 Imagine that you're a famous person (dead or alive). What is your main regret? See if other students can guess who you are.

3 *A* You're in favour of nuclear power.
*B* You're against nuclear power.
*C* You're a TV interviewer. Interview A and B for a TV documentary.

# Conversational English

## 1 Making offers

That's very kind of you. My hands are rather dirty.

No, that's OK. I can hear it all right.

No thanks. I don't mind walking.

Yes, thanks. I'd love some.

Well, I'd love to, but I'm busy that evening.

Shall I ...?
I'll ... if you like.
Would you like me to ...?

Do you want (to) ...?
Would you like (to) ...?

1 Here are some replies to offers. What offer do you think the other person made? Use expressions from the box.

Now listen to the conversations.

2 Work in pairs.

*Student A*

B has got a lot of problems, and you want to help. Decide what you could do to help B with each problem.

Now get together with B. Keep making offers until you offer what B wants.

You've been thrown out of your flat.

You've hardly got any money.

If you find somewhere to live, you don't know how you can move all your things.

You haven't had a good meal for days.

The whole thing has made you ill and exhausted.

*Student B*

You've got a lot of problems, but A is going to help you. For each problem, decide exactly *how* you'd like A to help you.

Now get together with A. Keep refusing A's offers until he/she offers what you want.

## Talking points

**Choose one of these topics. Take it in turns to say a sentence or two about it.**

**It's ages since ...**

**Getting old**

**Young people and the law**

**Things I can never remember**

**Showing your feelings**

**I'd be happier if ...**

**Regrets**

**Are human beings an endangered species?**

## Words

1 **Complete these questions:**
- What .......... ice-cream do you want?
- What .......... shoes do you take?
- What .......... car do you drive?

2 **Look at these remarks. What's happening?**
- 'There's no need to get so angry.'
- 'Don't cry. It'll all turn out all right.'
- 'No. I've already told you. I won't do it.'

3 **Continue these lists:**
- wedding, bridgegroom ...
- funeral, coffin ...
- global warming, desertification ...

## 2 In the street

1 *a* **Complete the questions in these conversations.**

**Now listen to the recording.**

*b* **Make these questions more polite.**
- Where's the station?
- What time does the bank open?
- Is there a bookshop near here?
- Where can I buy a newspaper?

2 **Think of a polite question to ask someone in the street outside your school. See how many people know the answer.**

# Additional material

## 13·Focus on Form·1 *Facts*

## 24·3 Endangered species: *pandas*

- Pandas are one of the rarest animals in the world. They live only in a small area in the mountains of South-western China.
- There are only 500–1,000 pandas surviving in the wild, and the number is decreasing all the time. There are about 100 more in zoos and research stations.
- Although they are protected, pandas are still poached for their skins. Because they are so rare, their skins are very valuable.
- Pandas live in mountain forests, and can only eat bamboo. As their habitat is getting smaller and smaller, pandas are in danger of dying from lack of suitable food.
- Zoos are making efforts to breed pandas in captivity, but this is very difficult. Also, baby pandas weigh only 100 grams at birth, so they need to be looked after very carefully. Since 1963 about 50 baby pandas have been born in captivity, and around half of them are still alive today.

## 15·Focus on Form·2 *Student A*

**This is last week's news. Find out from B what has happened since then.**

There were worries last night about the safety of the Claxton nuclear power station, after reports of leaks

**The search is continuing in the French Alps for a party of schoolchildren who failed to return from a**

There are rumours that the Louvre is planning to sell the priceless Mona Lisa, the most

A group of 200 refugees crossed the border last night without passports or visas and

**Police were questioning billionaire Oliver James last night about the disappearance of millions of dollars**

The Government has denied that Miss Botham is a spy, and has demanded that she should be released immediately and

Only 3,000 tickets have so far been sold for the 'Rock Show of the Century' due to take place

## 17·Focus on Form·3 *Student A*

## 24·3 Endangered species: *tigers*

- There are six species of tiger still in existence. They are found in Siberia, India and South-east Asia.
- 50 years ago, tigers were common throughout much of Asia, living in many different habitats from tropical forest to semi-desert.
- Because people thought they were dangerous, they were hunted and trapped, and tiger skins were considered very valuable.
- By 1970, there were fewer than 5,000 tigers left, and many of their habitats had been destroyed.
- In 1972, Operation Tiger was launched: tigers were protected by law and reserves were created to protect the species.
- Gradually, numbers began to increase, and there are now some 8,000 tigers living in the wild.

## 17·Focus on Form·3 *Student B*

## 15·Focus on Form·2 *Student B*

**This is today's news. Answer A's questions using the Present perfect tense, active or passive.**

## 24·3 Endangered species: *rhinos*

- Most rhinos live in Africa. There are two African species: the black rhino, which lives in East Africa and the white rhino, which is found in Southern Africa. There are also a few rhinos in Asia, mainly in India.
- Over the last 20 years, numbers of rhinos have dropped rapidly: there are now fewer than 10,000 in the whole world, and the number is still falling.
- The main threat to rhinos is from poachers, who hunt them for their 'horns', which are in fact made of stiff hair. The horns are sold in the Middle East, where they are used to make dagger handles, and also in the Far East, where they are used in medicines and aphrodisiacs.
- Trading in rhino horn is illegal, but it is still continuing. Unless more is done to protect them, they will almost certainly become extinct.

## 15·2 Tell me more

23 Morrison Drive
Redbridge

Monday 16th

Dear Lucy and Fred,

Just to let you know that the baby's arrived! It's a girl, and we've called her Frances, after Theresa's mother. She's a lovely baby, with blue eyes and black hair.

We went into hospital at 9 o'clock last night, when the labour started, and the baby was born just after 2 o'clock this morning – not bad! Theresa was wonderful. I was there the whole time, and the birth wasn't too difficult this time, thank goodness, although she's a big baby – nearly 4 kilos!

Theresa is fine, and sends her love. They're coming out of hospital on Friday, so do come and see us next week some time.

Henry's seen his little sister, and seems quite excited by the whole thing. I expect he'll change his mind before long!

See you soon.

Love,

David

## 24·3 Endangered species: *elephants*

- Elephants are found in Africa and in Asia (mainly India). African elephants are slightly larger and have much bigger ears.
- Elephants in Africa are in serious danger: nearly a million have been killed in the last 10 years, and only about 600,000 are left.
- In Asia, there are only about 50,000 elephants left in the wild. However, Asian elephants are used for transporting timber, so many are now born in captivity.
- Elephants are killed by poachers for their tusks, which they sell as ivory. Elephant ivory is made into ornaments, piano keys, chopsticks and other objects.
- In 1989, governments of 79 countries agreed to ban all trade in ivory, and this ban came into effect in 1990. Unfortunately, as long as people buy ivory, poaching will continue and elephants will be in danger.

# Tapescripts

## *13·1* National differences

1 In France most of the people want to have a very long time for lunch. In Britain it doesn't seem to be important because people take a cup of tea and a very quick sandwich and it's OK.
2 Another very surprising thing for the foreigner is the way the people obey the law – you seem to have much more discipline than in France, and you respect the police much more than we do. For instance, people park their car everywhere, and they know it is forbidden but they do it – in Britain people don't do that.
3 In England it's easier to feel alone, people don't bother you, don't look after you or worry about you so much, so it's easy to get sort of, to get lost or to hide away here. When you're in the United States people want to know who you are, they tend to speak to you, to find out who you are, what you're doing.
4 Yes, one thing I should mention is that the United States is I think a much more exciting place to be than England, but there is a drawback and that is, you do have this sense of danger in the United States, especially in big cities, that you don't get so much in England or Britain as a whole. You feel safe in England.
5 Japanese houses are really small and people live close to each other, and there aren't so many parks, there aren't so many places where you can play when you are little, and it's very difficult for people to relax.
6 Japan is quite safe, and you can leave your handbag behind when you leave the room without being really careful about it. But in Britain you really have to keep eye on your handbag when you leave the room, and you have to take it with you when you leave.

## 14·2 Changing channels

And our next guest has come all the way from the United States to be with us tonight. Ladies and gentlemen, Michael Douglas!

It is not yet clear exactly how the accident happened, but police believe that the lorry driver swerved to avoid a child. The driver is ...

*(Sound of cars and guns)*

It's amazing to think that I am standing at the very spot where, two and a half thousand years ago, the Athenian and Persian armies met at the battle of Marathon. Since then, of course, ...

And as they come into the last lap, it's still the Kenyan way out in front, and if he can keep this up he could be on his way to a new world record. And ...

Aw, you wouldn't want to shoot a friendly little rabbit now, would you? ...

- Samantha – your question for £200. What is a *didgeridoo*?
- A kind of bird?
- Come in. Oh. It's you. What do you want?
- I just ... wanted to say I was sorry about yesterday.
- A bit late for that, isn't it?

Hello? Anyone here? Hello?

## 14·4 Easy listening

1 Sometimes in the mornings I use it as an alarm clock. It's got three different timers and the first alarm that goes off usually starts off with the seashore and seagulls and I listen to that for about 15 minutes. And the next one comes on which is, wakes me up a bit more is more like south-east Asian pop music. And then I get the World Service news at 8 o'clock in the morning to finally wake me up.

2 Also there are these *karaoke* channels, about maybe four or five of them I think. And *karaoke* is the thing where you sing along to background music and you have a microphone and you can become a pop star for a few minutes and sing along to the music so I use this a lot now. I've learnt a few of the Japanese songs now. I can sing maybe five or six of them.

3 About the alibi channels, I did actually use one once. I'd been out quite late one night and overslept and was late for work. So I just got hold of the radio, flipped onto the alibi channel, which is the sound of, sounds as though you're in a phone box in the street with passing cars and sort of horns going. And I turned it up fairly loud, put my telephone next to it and explained to the secretary at work that I was on my way to the office and I'd been to a meeting which started at 8.30 in the morning.

4 Also there are various kinds of music, you can get Indian music and Mexican music for example. So when I'm at home cooking and cooking a Mexican meal and I get my friends to come over and we put the Mexican channel on so it creates a nice atmosphere for dinner.

## 15·1 In the news

The news at 6 o'clock.

The body of American TV presenter Clive Robbins has been found off the coast of Florida. Mr Robbins was reported missing two days ago when he failed to appear for breakfast on his yacht while on holiday in the Florida Keys. The body was found shortly after 6 o'clock this morning by a rescue helicopter, and was flown immediately to Miami for a post-mortem examination.

Two people have been killed in an explosion which badly damaged a house in South-east London early this afternoon. First reports say that the explosion was caused by a bomb, and a number of bombs and other weapons have been found in the house. Police believe that a group of terrorists were using the house as a weapons store, and that the bomb went off accidentally.

And finally, thieves got a nasty surprise when they stole a van from a motorway service station yesterday afternoon. When they finally opened the van, which belongs to the Kent Wildlife Park, they found two tigers inside, which were on their way to the Wildlife Park from London Zoo. The thieves, obviously animal lovers, immediately phoned the Wildlife Park, who have now recovered their van – and the tigers – unharmed.

## 15·4 Eavesdropping

*Part 1*

A I don't think you can blame me just because you've been sleeping badly. It's hardly my fault, is it?

B I didn't blame you, I didn't, I never blamed you, I just said I'm, I think I'll go to bed early because I've not, you know, I didn't sleep very well.

A Yeah OK but you seem to imply that just because I'm not working that somehow I'm just you know sitting around doing nothing.

B I just said I was going to bed early because I was very tired. I slept very badly last night, I'm tired, I've got a busy, you know, busy day ahead of me.

A Oh, oh and I haven't. (Well) Because I'm just going to be sitting around watching television and twiddling my thumbs.

B I didn't say that, did I? Look I'm sorry you haven't got enough to do. I'm sorry that you're bored.

A I've got plenty to do, thank you very much. I've been out looking for five different jobs.

*Part 2*

1 A We've just got to do something. I mean she came home again after midnight last night.
B I know, she hasn't looked at a book for weeks. She's never going to pass her exams at this rate.

2 A I bet you'll be glad to see them go, won't you?
B Yeah, it's exhausting, I mean it's nice to see them because they live so far away, but, well it is hard work.

3 A He's so different. He used to be so shy and quiet.
B I know, it really is incredible. I think he's changed since his divorce, don't you?

## 16·1 In the classroom

1 We sat in the dark and we watched these slides of different paintings and monuments and it was quite enjoyable.

2 We learnt a lot of dates and we learnt a lot about battles and kings and queens but we never learnt anything about ordinary people who had lived ordinary lives.

3 We did a lot of singing but if you wanted to learn to play an instrument you had to pass a special test.

4 I think my teachers mostly focused on grammar, but we also had the chance to speak in, during the class.

5 I remember we had a map of the world and we used to spin it around and wherever we put our finger on we used to study the country wherever our finger had landed.

6 We had the chance to do a lot of our own experiments which was very good because it gave you the opportunity to see how things worked.

7 We had a very good teacher and we used to write a lot of stories and a lot of poems and I really enjoyed writing poetry. That was great.

## 16·3 Going through the system

A At what age do children start school in the States?

B Generally six. That's when I started.

A And that goes up to what age?

B That goes up to grade six, so that would be what? Twelve years old? And then you go to seventh grade in Junior High School, in fact you go for three years to a Junior High School, 7th, 8th and 9th grades.

A And then you go to real High School?

B And then comes the real thing, three years of High School. That's the 10th, the 11th and 12th grades.

A And that takes you up to what age? Sixteen or ...?

B Seventeen, eighteen. It's quite

common to finish High School with your Diploma at age seventeen.

A And how many subjects do you take for your Diploma?

B Well that depends on what type of Diploma you're doing. There are really two types – there's an academic Diploma, which would prepare you for College, and there's a non-academic Diploma, which is more vocationally orientated. Both types of Diploma have their compulsory subjects, you know, like in the academic Diploma you have to do English. But then in both cases again the student has some choice, so in addition there are what's called 'electives'.

A 'Electives' means you can choose the subject ...?

B Exactly, exactly. So in the United States you could do a credit in driving, for example, and learn to drive at High School. Or typing is another skill that you can learn in High School, and that will count towards your Diploma.

## 16·4 Improve your memory

A OK I gather you've got an interesting way of learning words in a foreign language.

B Yes it's actually a very easy way of learning foreign words. What you do is to, you think of a word in your own language, in my case English, which sounds something like the word you're trying to learn and then you just imagine a picture in your mind which links the two ideas – the idea of the foreign word and the idea of the English word.

A Can you give me an example?

B Yeah, an easy example is the Greek word *skylos* which means 'dog'. And this immediately reminds me of the English words *ski* and *loss*, so I just imagine a picture of a skier on a mountain, one of his skis has come off and he's lost it and there's a dog carrying it back to him in his mouth. An example from a different language might be the Japanese word for 'thank you' which is *arigato*. Now that sounds to me a little bit like *alligator*, so I could imagine a rather unpleasant picture of somebody whose leg has just been eaten by an alligator and the alligator's smiling and saying 'Thank you very much.'

A OK I'm going to try you out with some words in Russian (Goodness. Russian, yeah) You don't know Russian, do you?

B No no no.

A OK. Well here's the Russian word for 'teacher', which is *uchitelj*.

B Could you say it again?

A *Uchitelj*.

B *U-chit-elj*. Oh that's easy. The middle of this word is the English word *cheat*, which is something we often associate with teachers and students. So I can imagine a student sitting in an examination and he's cheating, he's copying from the student sitting next to him. And the teacher is standing over him saying 'You cheat!'

A OK, here's another word. It's the Russian word for 'fire' which is *ogonj*. *Ogonj*.

B *Ogonj*. Mm. Oh yes, again, let's take the middle of the word, *gone*. We think of a fire perhaps that's gone out. So I just imagine a picture of a fire in a fireplace and it's gone out. Easy.

A OK. Thank you. I'll try it as a technique.

## 17·4 The dead rabbit

Well, this friend of mine had a dog, which he'd bought for his daughter's tenth birthday. This dog was always getting into trouble, and it had already completely wrecked their house and dug up their garden.

Anyway, one Friday this dog turned up with a dead rabbit in its mouth, which it brought into the house and dropped on the floor. And my friend's daughter immediately recognised this rabbit as the one that belonged to the little boy next door, and the little boy kept this rabbit in a hutch in his garden, so the dog must have got into their garden and killed it.

So my friend had a look at the rabbit, which was all muddy and dirty, but it didn't seem to have any tooth marks on it and it wasn't damaged in any way. So he had an idea.

What he did was he cleaned the rabbit up and he dried it with a hairdryer, and made it look really nice, and then later on that night when the neighbours had gone to sleep, he slipped over the garden fence and put the dead rabbit back in its hutch. The next morning there was a ring at the doorbell, and it was the little boy's mother, and she was looking really upset. And my friend said 'What's the matter?'

And she said 'It's terrible. It's little Timmy's rabbit. I just can't understand it. The rabbit died two days ago, and so we took it out of its hutch and buried it in the garden, and this morning he went back out into the garden to clean out the rabbit hutch so we could sell it – and there was the rabbit back in the hutch.'

## 18·3 Guilty or not guilty?

And now the swordstick trial. Mr Edward Cook has been found guilty of carrying an offensive weapon. He was given a 28-day suspended prison sentence, and fined £200. He was also ordered to pay £2,500 towards the costs of the trial, and to hand over his swordstick to the police. Afterwards, Mr Cook said he was shocked at the verdict, and repeated that he had only used the swordstick in self-defence. 'I had to use it,' he told reporters, 'or I'd be a dead man today.'

## 18·4 Detective Shadow

A *(Reading)* There was a loud crack of thunder and the power went off. Shadow started to look for a candle when he heard a knock at his door. It was Harry Fox, who lived nearby with his uncle. 'Come quickly!' cried Harry Fox. 'My Uncle Cecil has been shot!' Shadow grabbed a torch and ran to his neighbour's house. When they arrived, Shadow shone the light on Cecil's face, and he knew immediately that he was dead. Harry explained that he and his uncle had been watching TV, when suddenly the window had smashed in and Cecil had fallen forward dead. 'At that moment there was a crash of thunder and the power went out,' Harry said. 'That's when I ran and got you.' Just then the power returned and the two reading lights in the room came on. Shadow and Harry sat in total silence for two minutes, unable to believe the terrible scene before them. Shadow finally turned to Harry and said,'Your story is obviously completely untrue.' Why does Shadow think Harry's lying?

B So right. So Shadow was in his house (Mm) and Harry Fox and his uncle were nearby, they're neighbours (Mm-hm) ...

B ... Erm, they sat in silence. So the television didn't come on then when the power came on.

A No.

B Ah, right. So in other words Harry had been lying. And that's how Shadow knew, because Harry had said they were watching the television. If they were watching the television, it would have come on again. So, is that right?

A Absolutely right, yes (Good). If Harry Fox and his Uncle Cecil were watching TV, as Harry claimed, the TV should have come back on when the power returned. They sat in silence for a couple of minutes, so it was obvious that the TV had not been on.

B Been on. Ah, OK, yeah.

A Well done.

## Making choices

1 A What about this one? Is that the kind of thing you have in mind?

B Um, no, I'd prefer something a little darker.

A Mm. Well, there's this one.

B Yes, that's better. I'll have that one.

2 A Come on. Are you ready?

B Um, actually, I don't think I'll come, if you don't mind. I'd rather get on with this book.

3 A I'll have the chicken, please.
B One chicken ... And for you sir?
A I'd like the lamb, please.

4 A Well we could drive. Or would you rather go by train?
B Well actually, I'd prefer to fly, if we can afford it.

## 19·3 It's a long time since ...

1 When I was in France I used to go dancing every, every week, and I haven't been dancing since September, which is several months now. And I really miss it because I would go there every Monday, I remember. So I'm just quite looking forward to doing it again when I go back to France.

2 The last time I played football was when I used to live in South Africa, because it was quite warm and we used to play all year round, it was never cold or anything like that, so that was quite fun. That was about seven years ago that I really, really enjoyed playing football all the time. Then when I moved to England it was a lot colder, and we had to play football in the cold, in shorts, and it was freezing, so I didn't really enjoy it then and I gave it up quite soon after that.

3 It's two years since I last went ice-skating, and I used to really enjoy ice-skating because you could go with a big group of friends, and you could go for a long time, about three hours. But I haven't been for a very long time now because it's got more expensive and because I don't seem to have very much time.

## 20·1 Birth, marriage and death

1 After the burial it's very traditional to celebrate the death. And we celebrate that by eating and drinking and in some cases singing traditional Irish songs. Because we consider it to be a happy occasion, especially if the person is old, and they've, they're going to heaven and they're going to be rewarded in the afterlife.

2 The bride is dressed up and she sits in a chair surrounded by flowers and children, and everybody troops past to have a look at her. And then you just sit down, and you're given lots of sweets and drinks, soft drinks. And then the groom and his entourage arrive, and he takes her hand and leads her away.

3 In Scotland, there's a tradition related to birth, where you must present the baby with a piece of silver, a silver coin. And you have to take this coin and actually place it in the baby's hand and make the baby hold it. The idea behind this is that the baby will be rich in later life.

4 After the death of the person, this person's corpse will be taken to the furnace, where the corpse is cremated. And afterwards from the furnace bones are taken out. And all the family members get together to pick up the bones with chopsticks. Each relative takes one bone and put them in a small jar, and we bury it.

5 The bride is dressed in white and the bridegroom is dressed in a black suit and white shirt. At midnight she goes away and takes off her white dress and puts on a red dress. She comes back to dance with the guests, and the guests pay for dancing with her, so she dances with everybody and when she's ready and when the bridegroom thinks that's enough, then he takes her by the hand and they run away and they take all the money with them.

## 20·4 A Good Boy,Griffith

*Section 5*

The next afternoon he went up the hill to the red brick cottage again. He saw the lace curtains move suddenly as he approached, and the door opened before he had even time to reach the knocker.

'Come back?' she asked. 'If you've not got the money you might as well turn around and go.'

'Steady, steady, girl,' said Griffith, 'don't get so jumpy. I've got the money. Have you got the ring?'

He took the roll of white notes from his waistcoat pocket. 'Come on in then,' she said.

With a quick turn she walked from the room and he heard her going up the stairs. Then she came slowly down.

'There's your ring,' she said, half throwing it on the table. 'Keep it. I'd rather have the money.'

Griffith took the ring. 'One more thing,' he said. 'Nobody must know.'

'All right,' she said quietly. 'Morgan didn't even know I had the thing. I told him I'd given it back to you.'

*Section 6*

When Morgan came home he washed the grease from his hands under the tap then sat down to his meal. Blodwen poured the tea unsteadily.

'What's up, Blod?' he said. 'You don't look so good, girl.'

'I'm all right,' she said.

'Was Griffith here today?' he said casually, cutting a thick slice from the loaf.

She went pale but he did not look up. 'Yes,' she admitted.

He laughed. 'Good boy, Griff, you know. Sort of steady chap. Can't see why you didn't marry him. Always trust him.'

'Does it matter now?'

'No,' he replied good-humouredly. 'The thing is, did he bring the fifty quid?'

Blodwen felt her heart capsize. 'Yes,' she said shakily. 'Yes, he did ...'

Her husband nodded. 'Good boy, Griff. Came in and asked me to lend it to him so he could get a real special ring for his girl Gwen. Nice girl. Said he'd get it from his savings when his dad came home from the pit and bring it up here. A good boy, Griff; yes a good boy ...'

## 21·3 Getting to know you

1 A Hi. Which class are you in?
B I'm studying Japanese.
A Oh, I'm in the same class. (Ah) Yeah, I've just joined, this is my first time. Are you enjoying it?
B Yes, I am. It's fine.
A Have you ever been to Japan?
B I've been once, yes.

2 A Hi. I'm Ian. Do you know anyone here?
B Only a few people. Oh, I'm Alison. (Hi) Do you know anyone here?
A Er just Bob, who I, I think it's his party actually, he met me when he came in.
B Yes. Are you from the States?
A No, I'm from Canada, but you know, it's sort of the same accent, but I'm Canadian, actually.

3 A Excuse me, how long have you been waiting?
B Um, about half an hour now. These buses are always late.
A Are you going to town?
B Yes, yes I am.
A Are you going shopping?
B Er no, I'm meeting a friend there.

## 21·4 Tags

1 It's a bit cold today, isn't it?
2 They speak Arabic in Iran, don't they?
3 You haven't seen my glasses, have you?
4 Auckland isn't the capital of New Zealand, is it?
5 They didn't stay very long, did they?
6 That film was awful, wasn't it?
7 Penguins can't fly, can they?

## 22·2 Reactions

1 A Happy birthday, Annie.
B Oh thank you! Can I open it now?
A Of course.
B Oh it's lovely. Thank you very much.

2 A What's the matter?
B My girlfriend Mary just walked right by me in the street and didn't even say hello.
A Maybe she didn't see you.
B She saw me all right. She's just, I don't know, mad at me or something.
A I'm sure she isn't darling – don't get too worried about it. She probably just didn't see you.

3 A Do you want to go for a walk?
B No I've got far too much work to do.
A Oh please, it's a lovely day.
B I know, but let's go later, eh?

4 A Would you mind keeping the noise down, please? I'm trying to get to sleep, I've got to get up early in the morning, this has been going on for two hours.
B Yeah well I'm sorry. It's just, a friend of mine's just got married, you see. We're having a party.
A Ah well I hope he's very happy. The thing is I've got to get up early. When are you going to stop?

5 A Is anything the matter?
B It's Caroline. She's left me.
A Oh no. I don't believe it. What happened?
B Oh nothing really happened. She just said she was moving out and she didn't want to see me any more. I think she's met someone else.
A Oh that's terrible. Look, tell you what, I'll make us some coffee, and then we'll get in the car and go for a drive.

## 22·4 What's in a smile

A So you've just been on a smile therapy course. What was it like?
B It was really good. I enjoyed it.
A What did you have to do on the course?
B We started off by doing breathing exercises so we could feel about breathing in happiness and of course we had to smile, we had to smile a lot, and the idea is that if you smile you feel better, it puts you in a good mood, so we tried that. We had to try to remember the last time we felt happy and think about that feeling. Then we were given a lecture and that helped to explain how we forget to laugh. When we grow up we forget to laugh. As children you play and you laugh and you smile and you have fun and as you get older life is much more serious. And they're trying to help us to go back to that feeling of childhood and the fun that we had.
A So did you do any activities on the course?
B Yes, they got us into groups, and we had to think back to things that had made us laugh. That was really interesting because it's surprising how there's some people who just can't remember what last made them laugh.
A What about you? Could you remember?
B Oh yes I could remember because I watch funny things on the telly.
A And what else happened on the course?
B Well, the last bit was really the best. That's when they put on a tape of somebody laughing and they were just laughing really out of control and it was really good because we all started to laugh and one by one everybody was laughing because laughing is infectious and that was really good fun.
A What about homework? Do you do anything at home in between the sessions?
B Oh yes, we have this homework to do. We have to practise to laugh. It sounds a bit strange at first, you have to stand in front of the mirror and laugh, sort of like laugh at yourself, which the first time feels embarrassing but it does work and it makes you feel better. Yes. It's good.
A So in general do you think the course has helped to make you feel better about yourself?
B Yeah I do and it is good fun, and it's nice to be with a group, and I can think of some bad-tempered people who I would recommend should go on it.

## 23·1 Dilemmas

1 Well this is very difficult, but I'm vegetarian, and I don't think I could have eaten the flesh of another person. I don't think I could have lived with myself afterwards if I'd survived. So no, I wouldn't have eaten the flesh of another human being.

2 I think I would have eaten the flesh of the other passengers. If I looked at it from a point of view that I was one of the dead passengers, I wouldn't have minded my body helping other people live. So I think I would have reluctantly done it.

3 I think I probably would have ended up eating the flesh of my fellow passengers if I needed to to survive. I find the idea physically revolting when I think about it, but I don't find it morally revolting. I don't see any moral reason for not doing that if it's necessary to survive, so I probably would have done.

4 I would not have eaten the flesh of my fellow passengers, quite simply because I believe it's morally wrong to do so. So if it was a choice between starving to death and eating the body of another person, I would have chosen starvation.

## 24·4 The Doomsday Asteroid

1 Well if I only had one month left to live I'd certainly live it up. I'd spend every penny I have, I'd run up an enormous overdraft at the bank, buy everything I've ever wanted, eat anything I've ever wanted to eat, I don't care how bad it is for me – I'd just have a wild time.

2 I think I would go to Spain and get a really nice house on the beach, and have a month on the beach with my children, playing by the seaside, just having fun.

3 I'd buy a wonderful pair of walking boots and an enormous rucksack, and set off with my partner to walk around the entire coast of the British Isles and just stick to the coast, and just keep going, until the end.

4 Well it isn't absolutely certain that the world would end in six months, so I think I'd probably just carry on as normal really. But I think I'd try and do all those things that I've always wanted to do that I've never done. Like I'd learn to fly, and I'd try parachute-jumping, and I think I'd like to go scuba-diving. And that's what I'd do. I'd live normally, but I'd make sure that I really filled up my time with enjoyable things.

5 I suppose in such a situation, most people would just want to travel around. So I would open a travel agency and organise trips to the most exotic places, just like palm beaches, and exotic islands, visiting relations, and so on and so forth. And I would just earn a fantastic amount of money. There is a 30% chance that the asteroid wouldn't hit the Earth, so I'd become just fantastically rich. And when everybody goes to work after the panic has gone I would just retire and enjoy myself.

## Making offers

1 A Would you like me to open the door for you?
B That's very kind of you. My hands are rather dirty.

2 A Shall I turn the volume up a bit?
B No, that's OK. I can hear it all right.

3 A I'll give you a lift to the station if you like.
B No thanks. I don't mind walking.

4 A Do you want some cream on it?
B Yes, thanks. I'd love some.

5 A Would you like to come to a concert on Friday?
B Well I'd love to, but I'm busy that evening.

## In the street

1 A Excuse me. Do you know if there's a Post Office near here?
B Yes. There's one just round the corner.

2 A Excuse me. I wonder if you could tell me what the time is.
B Yes. It's nearly half past three.

3 A Excuse me. Do you know if there's anywhere around here I can change some money?
B Well there's a bank in the next street.

4 A Excuse me. Can you tell me when the bus leaves?
B I think it goes in about ten minutes.

5 A Excuse me. Could you tell me the way to North Street?
B Yes. Carry on up here and it's the second on the left.

# Reference section

## 13 Comparing and evaluating

### Comparison of adjectives

- My car isn't nearly as fast = his car is much faster. (a big difference)
  My car isn't quite as fast = his car is slightly faster. (a small difference)

| His car is | much<br>far<br>a bit<br>slightly | faster<br>more expensive | than mine. |
|---|---|---|---|

| My car isn't | nearly<br>quite | as | fast<br>expensive | as his. |
|---|---|---|---|---|

- We can also make positive sentences with ... *as* ... *as*:
  I'm (just) *as* clever *as* you.
  She's nearly *as* tall *as* her mother.

### Comparison of adverbs

- If the adverb is formed by adding *-ly*, add *more*: quickly – more quickly; easily – more easily.
- If the adverb is the same as the adjective, add *-er*: hard – harder; fast – faster; early – earlier.
- Irregular: well – better.

### too and enough

| It was too | crowded.<br>noisy. |
|---|---|

| There | was<br>were | too | much noise.<br>many people. |
|---|---|---|---|

| It wasn't | fast<br>good | enough. |
|---|---|---|

| There | wasn't<br>weren't | enough | food.<br>people. |
|---|---|---|---|

- *too* is followed by an adjective or adverb, or by *much*/*many* + noun.
- *enough* comes after adjectives and adverbs, but before nouns.

### too/enough + infinitive

He was too ill. He couldn't go to work.
→ He was *too* ill to go to work.
The table was too heavy. I couldn't lift it.
→ The table was *too* heavy (for me) *to* lift.
(*not* ... ~~to lift it~~)
The water wasn't warm enough. We couldn't swim in it.
→ The water wasn't warm *enough* (for us) *to* swim in.

## 14 The media

- *The media* is a general term describing newspapers and magazines ('the Press') and radio and television. It is also called the *mass media*, because it brings information to large numbers of people.

### Newspapers and magazines

- You buy newspapers and magazines from a *newsagent* or *news-stand* (or, in some countries, from a *kiosk*).
- Most newspapers appear *daily* or *weekly* (*once a week*). Magazines are usually produced *weekly*, *fortnightly* (*once a fortnight*) or *monthly* (*once a month*).
- Newspapers contain *articles* and *features*, which are written by *journalists*. Usually they also have a *leading article* or *editorial*, which is written by the *editor* and gives the point of view of the newspaper.
- In many countries, the press is *independent*, and newspapers may be *right-wing* or *left-wing*. In some countries, the press is *controlled* by the state and may be *censored*.
- Typical contents of a newspaper:

| | |
|---|---|
| news | home news, foreign/international news, business/financial news, sports news |
| regular features | weather forecast, TV & radio programmes, horoscope, cartoons, letters, reviews, obituaries, advertisements, crossword |

### Radio and TV

- To listen to a radio programme, you *tune in* to the *station* (or *wavelength*) you want. When you watch TV, you choose the *channel* you want.
- Some types of TV programme and the people involved:

| Programme | People |
|---|---|
| news | newsreader |
| documentary | presenter |
| sports programme | commentator |
| chat show | host, guests |
| soap (opera) | actors |
| comedy show | comedian |

*Note: Chat show* is British English. In the USA it's called a *talk show*.

## 15 Recent events

### Present perfect simple tense

- We use the Present perfect simple to talk about recent events. It is often used for *announcing news* of something that has happened recently:
  Sarah *has got* engaged.
  There *has been* a plane crash at Heathrow Airport.
- If we want to focus on *what has happened* rather than on *who* has done the action, we often use the passive:
  A thief *has been arrested* (by the police).
  A new motorway *has been built*.
  (For tables of active and passive forms, see Unit 7.)

### Present perfect and past simple tenses

- We use the Present perfect when we are not interested in *when* things happened, but only in *the fact* that they have happened. If we mention *when* or *how*, we use the Past tense:
  Sarah *got* engaged at the weekend.
  A plane *crashed* at Heathrow Airport last night as it was coming in to land.
- In a single paragraph, it is common to use the Present perfect for *announcing* a piece of news, followed by the past tenses for *going into details*:
  There *has been* a plane crash at Heathrow Airport. The crash *took place* late last night as the plane *was coming* in to land. Five passengers *were killed* and ...

### Present perfect continuous tense

- We use the Present perfect continuous to talk about *recent activities*. It answers the question 'How have you been spending your time?':
  I*'ve been writing* letters.
  I *haven't been working* very hard.
- Like the Present perfect simple, this tense cannot be used with past time expressions, but we can use it with expressions such as *recently*, *this week*, *over the last few days*:
  I've been writing a lot of letters *recently*.
  I haven't been working very hard *this week*.
- Forms of the Present perfect continuous:

| | |
|---|---|
| I've<br>She's | been working hard. |
| Have you<br>Has she | been working hard? |

### Present perfect continuous and simple tenses

- Present perfect continuous and simple tenses are often used together. We use the continuous form to talk about *activities*, and the simple form to talk about individual *actions*:
  I*'ve been getting* ready for my trip. I*'ve packed* my case, *I've collected* my tickets and *I've changed* some money.
  I*'ve been writing* an essay. I*'ve written* it in rough but I *haven't typed* it out yet.

## 16 Teaching and learning

### School subjects

| Subject | Typical activities |
|---|---|
| languages | learning vocabulary; doing exercises; practising; translating |
| literature | reading novels, poetry, plays; writing essays |
| maths | making calculations; using tables |
| science | doing experiments |
| geography | using maps |
| history | learning dates; learning about governments, wars, leaders |
| art | painting, drawing |
| music | playing musical instruments |
| sport | playing football; doing athletics |

- You *go to* (or *attend*) school.
  You *study* or *do* school subjects (e.g. I never did French at school).
  You *take* or *sit* examinations (exams), and you either *pass* or *fail* them.

### Skills

- *good at* + *-ing* or noun.

| | | | |
|---|---|---|---|
| I'm | (very) good<br>quite good<br>not very good<br>no good | *at* | football.<br>French.<br>speaking French.<br>singing. |

- We can also say:
  I'm a good singer.
  She isn't a very good dancer.
- I *know how to* dance the tango. (= I can do it.)
  I *don't know how to* read music. (= I can't do it.)
  I *learnt how to* ride a horse when I was a child.

### Schools and universities

- British and American equivalents:

| GB | USA |
|---|---|
| nursery school | nursery school |
| primary school | grade school |
| secondary school | junior high school<br>high school |
| university | college |

- Before you leave school, you take a *school-leaving examination*. This qualifies you to go to *university*, where you study for a *degree*. When you get your degree, you *graduate* from university. Someone who has graduated from university is called a *graduate*.
  Note the pronunciation difference:
  to *graduate* /ˈgrædjʊeɪt/
  a *graduate* /ˈgrædjʊət/.

## 17 Narration

### Past perfect tense

- We use the Past perfect tense to *go back* from a point in the past to events that had happened *earlier*:
  I came home at 4 o'clock, but I was too late: my brother *had* already *left*.
  The woman opposite me looked very familiar; I was sure I'*d seen* her somewhere before.
- Active and passive forms:

| I<br>He | had(n't) | met them before. |
|---|---|---|

| The car | had(n't) been | serviced.<br>stolen. |
|---|---|---|

*I had*, *he had*, etc., are often shortened to *I'd*, *he'd*.

- Notice the relationship between *how things were* in the past and *what had happened* earlier:

| Past state | Previous event |
|---|---|
| The light *was* off. | Someone *had switched* the light off. |
| He *was* abroad. | He'*d gone* abroad. |
| There *wasn't* any hot water. | All the hot water *had been used* up. |

### Reported speech and thought

- Often we report what people said or thought in the past using verbs such as *said*, *told*, *discovered* and *realised*. When we do this, what the person actually said or thought usually changes *one tense further back*:
  'I'*m* French,' he said.
  → He said he *was* French.
  'I'*ve been* here before,' I thought to myself.
  → I realised that I'*d been* there before.
  'I'*ll* meet you at six,' she told me.
  → She told me she'*d* (= *would*) meet me at six.
- Tense changes in reported speech and thought:

| Actual words | | Reported |
|---|---|---|
| does | → | did |
| is doing | → | was doing |
| will do | → | would do |
| did<br>has done | → | had done |

- *say* and *tell*
  *say* is not followed by an object; *tell* is followed by an indirect object:
  He *said* he was French. (*not* ~~he said me~~)
  He *told me* he was French. (*not* ~~he told he was~~)
- Common reporting verbs:
  SPEECH: say, tell, explain, point out, reply, deny.
  THOUGHT: realise, discover, know, think.
- In certain cases (e.g. when reporting general facts or very recent speech) no tense change is necessary:
  Our teacher told us that penguins *live* in Antarctica.
  He said he'*ll* be there by 10 o'clock tonight.

## 18 Breaking the law

### Crimes and criminals

A *criminal* is someone who *commits* a *crime*.

| Crimes | | Criminals |
|---|---|---|
| *Verb* | *Noun* | |
| rob | robbery | robber |
| (burgle) | burglary | burglar |
| (steal) | thief | theft |
| murder | murder | murderer |
| kidnap | kidnapping | kidnapper |
| hijack | hijacking | hijacker |
| blackmail | blackmail | blackmailer |
| spy (on) | spying | spy |
| smuggle | smuggling | smuggler |
| (vandalise) | vandalism | vandal |

- You *steal* money or other things from people:
  He *stole* $100 *from* his cousin.
  They broke into our house and *stole* our TV.
  You *rob* people or places:
  They stopped him in a dark street and *robbed* him (of all his money).
  They *robbed* the National Bank.
- A *burglar* breaks into homes or shops and steals money or goods.
  A general word for someone who steals is a *thief*. The crime is *theft*.

### Punishments

- If you commit a minor offence (e.g. parking your car in the wrong place), you may have to *pay a fine* (= pay money).
  If you commit a more serious crime, you may *be sent to* (or *go to*) *prison*.
  In some countries, people are *sentenced to death* for serious crimes (e.g. murder).

### Trials

- The accused person *goes on trial* or *is tried* or *appears in court*.
- The *judge* is in charge of the trial.
  The *jury* decides if the accused is *guilty*.
  The *prosecution* tries to prove that the accused is guilty.
  The *defence defends* the accused.
  *Witnesses* give *evidence*.
- At the end of the trial, the jury give their *verdict* (either *guilty* or *not guilty*).
  If the accused is guilty the judge passes *sentence* (= decides on a punishment).

# 19 Up to now

### Present perfect tenses with for and since

- We use the Present perfect continuous to talk about the duration of activities that started in the past and are still going on now:
  I*'ve been travelling* for 3 days.
  He*'s been doing* the same job for 40 years.
- Some verbs are not normally used in the continuous form. With these verbs, we use the Present perfect simple:
  I*'ve had* this bicycle since I was a child.
  They*'ve been* here since Saturday.
- *for* is used with periods of time:
  for a year, for two weeks, for ages
  *since* is used with points of time:
  since 1950, since last week, since my birthday
  *since* can also be followed by a clause with a Past simple verb:
  I've been writing to her *since we met on holiday*.
  I've loved horses (ever) *since I was a child*.

### Origin and duration

- When we talk about activities or states continuing up to now, we can focus on when they *started* (*origin*) or on *how long* they've been going on (*duration*).
  ORIGIN: He *became* a teacher five years ago.
  DURATION: He*'s been* a teacher for five years.
  ORIGIN: They *started* building the dam in July.
  DURATION: They*'ve been building* the dam since July.
  Some common pairs of 'origin' and 'duration' verbs:

| | |
|---|---|
| become | be |
| buy/get | have |
| move to | live (in) |
| meet / get to know | know |
| learn (how to) | know (how to) |
| fall in love | be in love |
| die | be dead |

### How long …? and How long ago …?

- Questions with *How long ago …?* ask about *origin*:
  How long ago *did* you *meet* each other?
  – A year ago. / Last Christmas.
- Questions with *How long …?* ask about *duration*:
  How long *have* you *known* each other?
  – For a year. / Since last Christmas.

### Negative duration

- To express negative duration (how long something *hasn't* happened for), use the Present perfect simple:
  I *haven't visited* them for years.
  I *haven't spoken* French since I was at school.
  (*not* ~~I haven't been speaking~~ …)
- Other structures that express negative duration:
  – *The last time* I visited them *was* years ago.
  *The last time* I spoke French *was* at school.
  – *It's* years *since* I (*last*) *visited* them.
  *It's* three years *since* I (*last*) *spoke* French.

# 20 In your lifetime

### Birth, marriage and death

| Event | | Ceremony |
|---|---|---|
| *Noun* | *Verb* | |
| birth | be born | |
| | give birth (to) | |
| marriage | get married<br>marry | wedding |
| death | die | funeral |

- Before a baby is born, its mother is *pregnant*, or *is expecting a baby*. Then she *gives birth* (or *has the baby*), either in hospital or at home. A *midwife* helps to deliver the baby.
- In Britain and the US, many parents *christen* (= give a name to) or *baptise* their babies in church.
- At a wedding, the two people getting married are the *bride* and *bridegroom*. A wedding can be a *religious* ceremony (e.g. in church) or a *civil* ceremony (at a registry office). After the wedding, friends and relatives are invited to a *reception*. Then the couple go away on a *honeymoon*.
- When someone dies, the body is usually put into a *coffin*. At the funeral, the body may be *cremated* (= burnt) or *buried* in a *cemetery* (or *graveyard*). The *grave* is marked with a *gravestone* or *headstone*. Close relatives of the dead person usually go into *mourning*.

### Ages

| Person | Stage of life |
|---|---|
| child | childhood |
| adolescent/teenager | adolescence |
| adult/grown-up | adulthood |
| middle-aged person | middle age |
| old/elderly person | old age |

- an *adolescent* is someone who is *growing up* (between child and adult). A *teenager* is someone between 13 and 19.
- *adult*, *grown-up* and *adolescent* can be used as nouns or adjectives:
  He behaves like a grown-up.
  He behaves in a very grown-up way.
- *Elderly* is a polite way to refer to old people.
- Other ways of talking about age:
  She's *in her* (*early/mid/late*) *twenties*.
  She's a *seven-year-old* (child).

### Age and the law

In most countries, there is a *legal age* for certain activities.

- Often this is a *minimum age*:
  You *can't* drive a car *until* you are 17.
  You *have to* be 18 before you *can* vote.
- Or it may be a *maximum* age:
  You *have to* retire *at the age of* 65.

## 21 Finding out

### Information questions

- Questions with *What ...?*

| | |
|---|---|
| What | *kind of* bread shall I buy?<br>*type of* music does she like?<br>*make of* fridge have they got?<br>*colour* paper did you get?<br>*size* shoes does he wear?<br>*flavour* soup would you like? |

- *kind*, *type* and *make* are followed by *of*. Other category words are followed directly by another noun.
- Other questions with *What ...?*:
  What happened to your finger?
  What did you do to your finger?
  What happened to my coat? (= Where is it?)
- Questions with *How ...?*:
  – *How much/many, How long, How far, How often:*
  How much do you weigh?
  How far is it to the beach (from here)?
  – *How + adjective*:
  How expensive are the tickets?

### Indirect questions

| | |
|---|---|
| I wonder<br>I don't know | if they're here.<br>where they are. |
| Do you know | where they are? |

- Indirect questions have normal word order. Compare:
  DIRECT: *Does* she *live* here?
  INDIRECT: I wonder if she *lives* here.

### Reported questions

- As in reported speech (see Unit 17), the verb in a reported question changes one tense further back:
  '*Are* you French?'
  → He asked if I *was* French.
  '*Have* you *been* here before?'
  → She asked him if he'*d been* there before.
- Like indirect questions, reported questions keep normal word order:
  He asked me *where I lived*. (*not* ~~where did I live~~)

### Question tags

- We use question tags:
  – to check things when we're not quite sure:
  You don't eat beef, do you? (rising intonation)
  – to express an opinion or belief:
  It's cold in here, isn't it? (falling intonation)
- To form question tags, repeat the auxiliary verb:
  They*'re* coming tomorrow, *aren't* they?
  You *can* swim, *can't* you?
  With Present and Past simple sentences, use *do(n't)* or *did(n't)*:
  She works for IBM, *doesn't* she?

## 22 Speaking personally

### Feelings

| | | | |
|---|---|---|---|
| angry | embarrassed | jealous | upset |
| annoyed | excited | nervous | worried |
| depressed | frightened | relaxed | |

- *annoyed* = slightly angry.
  *nervous* = slightly afraid of something that's going to happen (e.g. an exam, a visit to the dentist).
  *upset* = very unhappy about something that's happened (you feel like crying).
- All these adjectives are used with *feel*, *get* and *make*:
  I *feel/get* frightened if I'm alone at night.
  Being alone at night *makes* me frightened.
- Adjectives ending in *-ed* have three equivalent forms:
  It *frightens* me.
  I makes me (feel) *frightened*.
  I find it *frightening*.

### Reporting verbs

Notice how we use these verbs to report conversations:
'Come on, cheer up – don't be sad.'
– I tried to *cheer* him *up*.
'OK, don't get angry – calm down.'
– I tried to *calm* her *down*.
'I'm very sorry.'
– I *apologised*.
'Go on – have a drink.'
– He tried to *persuade* me to have a drink.
'No, I don't want one.'
– I *refused* (to have one).
'This food's terrible.'
– She *complained* about the food.

### Reactions

*'Normal' adjectives:*

- With these adjectives we can use *very* or *quite*:
  The film was *very* disappointing.
  I found the film *quite* amusing.

| *Positive* | *Negative* |
|---|---|
| good<br>interesting<br>enjoyable<br>amusing<br>entertaining<br>exciting | bad<br>boring<br>dull<br>disappointing |

*'Extreme' adjectives:*

- *Wonderful*, *brilliant* and *terrific* all mean 'very good'. *Awful*, *dreadful* and *terrible* all mean 'very bad'.

| *Positive* | *Negative* |
|---|---|
| wonderful<br>brilliant<br>terrific<br>fascinating | awful<br>dreadful<br>terrible |

- Because these adjectives already have the sense of 'very', we can't use the word *very* with them. Instead we use *absolutely* for emphasis:
  The film was *absolutely* wonderful.
  I found the film *absolutely* terrible.
- We can use *really* with normal or extreme adjectives:
  The film was *really* | interesting. / fascinating.

# 23 The unreal past

## 'Unreal' conditionals

*2nd conditionals*

| If + past tense ... would/wouldn't (do) |
|---|

- We use the second conditional to imagine unreal things in the *present*:
  If I were rich, I'd give a lot of money to help poor people. (I'm not rich – I'm just imagining it.)
  She'd be happier if she had a more interesting job. (In fact she's *not* very happy and her job *isn't* very interesting.)
  (See also Unit 9.)

*3rd conditionals*

| If + past perfect tense ... would/wouldn't have (done) |
|---|

- We use the third conditional to imagine unreal things in the *past*:
  If I*'d known* you were alone, I *would have visited* you. (Unfortunately I *didn't* know, so I *didn't* visit you.)
  I *would have been* upset if they *hadn't invited* me to the party. (In fact they did invite me, so it was all right.)
- Notice that to form unreal conditionals, the verb moves *one tense back*. So to talk about the present, we use the *Past tense*; to talk about the past, we use the *Past perfect tense*.

*Mixed conditionals*

- We can mix second and third conditionals in one sentence. One part can refer to the present (second conditional) and one part to the past (third conditional):
  If you*'d remembered* to buy some petrol, we*'d be* home by now.
  (You *didn't* remember, so we*'re not* home now.)

## Expressing regret

- *I wish* + Past perfect tense is used for regretting past actions:
  I wish I*'d gone* to university. (I didn't go, and I regret it.)
  I wish I *hadn't shouted* at him. (I shouted at him, and now I'm sorry.)
  (For the use of *I wish* to make wishes about the present and future, see Unit 9.)
- *should(n't) have* + past participle is used for expressing regret or criticising past actions:
  I *should have* gone to university.
  I *shouldn't have* shouted at him.
  You *should have* told me. (You didn't tell me – that was wrong.)
  They *shouldn't have* stayed up so late. (They stayed up too late – now they're tired.)

# 24 Life on Earth

## Global issues

| Issues | Causes and effects |
|---|---|
| Air pollution | Factories, power stations and cars pollute the air → acid rain → trees are damaged. |
| Pollution of the sea | Industrial waste and sewage is dumped in the sea → wildlife is killed. |
| Global warming | Gases from cars and power stations → 'greenhouse effect' → the Earth becomes warmer → the climate changes → sea level rises. |
| Destruction of the rain forest | Trees are cut down → species become extinct, increases 'greenhouse effect'. |
| Nuclear power | Nuclear accidents → radioactive material escapes into the atmosphere → causes cancer. |
| Ozone layer | Chemicals destroy the ozone layer → sun causes skin cancer, damages crops. |
| Desertification | Overuse of farmland → desert spreads → farmland is lost. |

- Notice these verb/noun pairs:

| Verb | Noun |
|---|---|
| destroy | destruction |
| pollute | pollution |
| damage | damage (to) |
| protect | protection |

## Environmental action: verbs

- To help the environment:
  – *save* electricity; don't *waste* it
  – don't *use* more electricity than you need
  – *recycle* glass and paper; don't *throw* it *away*.
- Governments can *increase* or *decrease* (*raise* or *lower*) the price of certain products.
  They can *tax* (or *put a tax on*) products or *ban* them (= make them illegal).
- These are all things that can be done to *protect* the environment.

## Wildlife

- Animals, birds, fish and insects are forms of *wildlife*.
- Many animals that were once *common* have become *endangered species*: they are so *rare* that they could *become extinct*.
- Some animals are *hunted* for their meat or skins; others are in danger because their *habitat* is being destroyed.
- Many rare animals are *protected* by law (= it is illegal to kill them), and live in *wildlife reserves*; some also live *in captivity* (e.g. in zoos).

# Verb forms

## Verb tenses

Here is a summary of verb tenses taught in this book (numbers refer to units).

| | *Simple* | *Continuous* |
|---|---|---|
| *Present* | go/goes (1) | am/is/are going (1) |
| *Past* | went (3, 7, 19) | was/were going (3) |
| *Present Perfect* | have/has gone (7, 15, 19) | have/has been going (15, 19) |
| *Past Perfect* | had gone (17, 23) | (had been going) |
| *Future* | will go (11) | will be going (11) |
| *Future Perfect* | will have gone (11) | (will have been going) |
| *Conditional* | would go (9) | (would be going) |
| *Past Conditional* | would have gone (23) | (would have been going) |

## The Passive

The passive is formed with *be* + past participle. It can be in any tense: past, present or future:

**Present:** Wheat *is grown* all over Europe.
**Past:** They *were rescued* by helicopter.
**Present perfect:** The house *has been sold.*
**Past perfect:** I noticed that the lights *had been left* on.
**Future:** The road *will be opened* in six months' time.

The passive also has a continuous form, but this is commonly used only in the Present and Past tenses:

**Present:** My flat *is being redecorated.*
**Past:** He *was being questioned* by the police.

## Infinitives

The infinitive is the basic form of the verb. It is used after *to* and after modal verbs. There are four possible forms: present or past, simple or continuous:

| | *Simple* | *Continuous* |
|---|---|---|
| *Present* | work | be working |
| *Past* | have worked | have been working |

Examples:
Be quiet now – I want to *work.*
He's not at the office – he must *be working* at home today.
No wonder you failed the exam – you should *have worked* harder.
She's nearly 70, so she must *have been working* here for at least 50 years.

# Common functions

## Asking people to do things

– *Would you* pass the salt, please?
– *Could you* give me a lift to the station?
– *Would you mind* taking your shoes off?

## Asking permission

– *Can I* take my shoes off?
– *Do you mind if I* turn the radio on?
– *Is it all right if I* bring a friend?

## Making suggestions

– *Let's* go for a swim.
– *Why don't we* buy a CD player?
– *How about* (making) a cup of coffee?

## Giving advice

– *I think you should* go to bed earlier.
– *You'd better* tell the police immediately.
– *If I were you, I'd* complain about it.

## Deciding and choosing

– *I think I'll* buy a newspaper.
– *I'd like* an orange juice, please.
– *I'd rather* stay at home and watch TV.

## Making offers

– *Shall I* bring some food?
– *I'll* call a taxi *if you like.*
– *Would you like to* see my holiday photos?

## Asking for information

– *Can you tell me* what time the film starts?
– *Do you know* where I can find a dictionary?
– *I wonder if you could tell me* the way to the station.

# Irregular verbs

| *Infinitive* | *Simple past* | *Past participle* |
|---|---|---|
| be | was/were | been |
| beat | beat | beaten |
| become | became | become |
| begin | began | begun |
| bend | bent | bent |
| bite | bit | bitten |
| blow | blew | blown |
| break | broke | broken |
| bring | brought | brought |
| burn | burnt | burnt |
| build | built | built |
| buy | bought | bought |
| can | could | (been able) |
| catch | caught | caught |
| choose | chose | chosen |
| come | came | come |
| cost | cost | cost |
| cut | cut | cut |
| do | did | done |
| draw | drew | drawn |
| dream | dreamt | dreamt |
| drink | drank | drunk |
| drive | drove | driven |
| eat | ate | eaten |
| fall | fell | fallen |
| feed | fed | fed |
| feel | felt | felt |
| fight | fought | fought |
| find | found | found |
| fly | flew | flown |
| forget | forgot | forgotten |
| forgive | forgave | forgiven |
| freeze | froze | frozen |
| get | got | got |
| give | gave | given |
| go | went | gone (been) |
| grow | grew | grown |
| hang | hung | hung |
| have | had | had |
| hear | heard | heard |
| hide | hid | hidden |
| hit | hit | hit |
| hold | held | held |
| hurt | hurt | hurt |
| keep | kept | kept |
| know | knew | known |
| lay | laid | laid |
| lead | led | led |
| learn | learnt | learnt |
| leave | left | left |
| lend | lent | lent |
| let | let | let |
| lie | lay | lain |
| lose | lost | lost |
| make | made | made |
| mean | meant | meant |
| meet | met | met |
| pay | paid | paid |
| put | put | put |
| read | read | read |
| ride | rode | ridden |
| ring | rang | rung |
| rise | rose | risen |
| run | ran | run |
| say | said | said |
| see | saw | seen |
| sell | sold | sold |
| send | sent | sent |
| set | set | set |
| shake | shook | shaken |

| *Infinitive* | *Simple past* | *Past participle* |
|---|---|---|
| shine | shone | shone |
| shoot | shot | shot |
| show | showed | shown |
| shut | shut | shut |
| sing | sang | sung |
| sink | sank | sunk |
| sit | sat | sat |
| sleep | slept | slept |
| smell | smelt | smelt |
| speak | spoke | spoken |
| spell | spelt | spelt |
| spend | spent | spent |
| spread | spread | spread |
| stand | stood | stood |
| steal | stole | stolen |
| sweep | swept | swept |
| swim | swam | swum |
| swing | swung | swung |
| take | took | taken |
| teach | taught | taught |
| tear | tore | torn |
| tell | told | told |
| think | thought | thought |
| throw | threw | thrown |
| understand | understood | understood |
| wake | woke | woken |
| wear | wore | worn |
| win | won | won |
| write | wrote | written |

# Phonetic symbols

## Vowels

| *Symbol* | *Example* |
|---|---|
| /iː/ | tree /triː/ |
| /i/ | many /'meni/ |
| /ɪ/ | sit /sɪt/ |
| /e/ | bed /bed/ |
| /æ/ | back /bæk/ |
| /ʌ/ | sun /sʌn/ |
| /ɑː/ | car /kɑː/ |
| /ɒ/ | hot /hɒt/ |
| /ɔː/ | horse /hɔːs/ |
| /ʊ/ | full /fʊl/ |
| /uː/ | moon /muːn/ |
| /ɜː/ | girl /gɜːl/ |
| /ə/ | arrive /ə'raɪv/ |
| | water /'wɔːtə/ |
| /eɪ/ | late /leɪt/ |
| /aɪ/ | time /taɪm/ |
| /ɔɪ/ | boy /bɔɪ/ |
| /əʊ/ | home /həʊm/ |
| /aʊ/ | out /aʊt/ |
| /ɪə/ | hear /hɪə/ |
| /eə/ | there /ðeə/ |
| /ʊə/ | pure /pjʊə/ |

## Consonants

| *Symbol* | *Example* |
|---|---|
| /p/ | pull /pʊl/ |
| /b/ | bad /bæd/ |
| /t/ | take /teɪk/ |
| /d/ | dog /dɒg/ |
| /k/ | cat /kæt/ |
| /g/ | go /gəʊ/ |
| /tʃ/ | church /tʃɜːtʃ/ |
| /dʒ/ | age /eɪdʒ/ |
| /f/ | for /fɔː/ |
| /v/ | love /lʌv/ |
| /θ/ | thick /θɪk/ |
| /ð/ | this /ðɪs/ |
| /s/ | sit /sɪt/ |
| /z/ | zoo /zuː/ |
| /ʃ/ | shop /ʃɒp/ |
| /ʒ/ | leisure /'leʒə/ |
| /h/ | house /haʊs/ |
| /m/ | make /meɪk/ |
| /n/ | name /neɪm/ |
| /ŋ/ | bring /brɪŋ/ |
| /l/ | look /lʊk/ |
| /r/ | road /rəʊd/ |
| /j/ | young /jʌŋ/ |
| /w/ | wear /weə/ |

## Stress

We show stress by a mark (/'/) before the stressed syllable: later /'leɪtə/; arrive /ə'raɪv/; information /ɪnfə'meɪʃn/

# Acknowledgements

**The authors would like to thank the following for their contributions to *Language in Use* Intermediate:**

- for contributing to the listening and reading material: Carlos Aradas-Balbás, Carolyn Becket, Mª Celina Bortolotto, Jake Bundy, Lucy Bundy, Deb Clark, Bryan Cruden, James Dingle, Maria Dingle, Kayoko Enomoto, Jahel Fabris, Amy Fisher, David Fisher, Colette Fitzpatrick, Véronique Foray, Genevieve Higgins, Laura Jerran, Sakae Katoh, Catriona Maclachlan, Jonathan Mullan, Sally Mullan, Mike Mendenhall, Alan Ogilvy, Shane Pope, Helen Sandiford, Ewa Simbieda, Aileen Smith, Carsten Williams, Ingrid Williams, Jan Williams, Larissa Williams, Tony Williams, Gabriela Zaharias; and all the actors whose voices were recorded in studio sessions.
- for the production of the recorded material: Martin Williamson (Prolingua Productions), Peter Taylor (Taylor Riley Productions Ltd.), and Peter and Diana Thompson (Studio AVP).

**The authors would also like to thank the following at Cambridge University Press:**

- Colin Hayes for his continuing support and help.
- Peter Donovan for organising and steering the project through its various stages.
- Nick Newton and Anne Colwell for organising and overseeing design and production.
- Joanne Currie for her excellent design.
- Catherine Boyce for her work on the Pilot edition.
- Molly Bannister, Sue Featherstone and Val Grove for general administrative help.
- James Dingle, our Editor, for his tireless dedication, constructive ideas and good judgement.

**The authors and publishers would like to thank the following institutions and teachers for their help in testing the material and for the invaluable feedback which they provided:**

A.C.T., Paris, France; Rowan Ferguson, Executive Language Services, Paris, France; Lanser SA, Paris, France; The British Council, Athens, Greece; John Eaglesham, British School, Milan, Italy; Centro Linguistico di Ateneo, Parma University, Parma, Italy; Ridge International, Osaka, Japan; Tessa Pacey, ILC, Tokyo, Japan; Sunshine College Tokyo, Japan; Janaka Williams, Simul Academy, Kyoto, Japan; Lexis, Granada, Spain; LinguaSec, Madrid, Spain; Joe Hogan, The House, Palafrugell, Spain; English 1, Seville, Spain; Istanbul Technical University, Istanbul, Turkey; Özel Eyüboğlu Lisesi, Istanbul, Turkey; Roger Scott, Bournemouth, UK.

**The authors and publishers are grateful to the following copyright owners for permission to reproduce copyright material. Every endeavour has been made to contact copyright owners and apologies are expressed for any omissions.**

pp. 30–1: Times Editions Pte Ltd for texts adapted from *Britain*, *Singapore*, *Spain* and *Thailand* in the *Culture Shock* series, published by Kuperard (London) Ltd; The Rough Guides for text adapted from *The Rough Guide to West Africa*; p. 38: advertisements and Yellow Pages cover reproduced by kind permission of BT Yellow Pages. 'Yellow Pages' is a registered trademark of British Telecommunications plc in the United Kingdom; pp. 40–1: GE Magazines for text adapted from 'HELP! nobody loves us!' from *Me*, 10 July, 1989; pp. 48–9: John Murray (Publishers) Ltd for pictures and text adapted from *Victorian Inventions* by Leonard de Vries, 1991; p. 50: Simon & Schuster, Inc. for text adapted from *The Great Reckoning*, © James Dale Davidson and Lord William Rees-Mogg, 1993; p. 57: *Daily Record* and *Daily Mail*, © *Daily Mail* / Solo, for adapted text; p. 64: *The Beano*, © D. C. Thomson & Co. Ltd., *Car Magazine*, *Hello!*, *Homes and Gardens* and *Reader's Digest* for permission to reproduce covers; p. 66: *The Times* for text adapted from 'Easy Listening' by Joanna Pitman from *The Times* 22 May, 1992, © Times Newspapers Ltd. 1992; pp. 74–5: Multimedia for text adapted from *Your Memory, A User's Guide* by Alan Baddeley, © Multimedia Books Limited, published in the UK by Pelican and USA by Prion; p. 81: *The Times* for text adapted from 'Passenger "stabbed attacker on Tube with swordstick"'from *The Times* 10 September, 1987, © Times Newspapers Ltd. 1992. The names have been changed to protect those involved in the case; pp. 82–3: MindTrap Games Inc. for texts adapted from the board game *MindTrap*, © MindTrap Games Inc.; p. 93: Leslie Thomas for *A Good Boy, Griffith* , © Leslie Thomas; p: 100: *The Observer* for text from 'The medicine' by Thomas Quirke, © *The Observer*; p. 101: Little, Brown and Co. (UK) Ltd. for text adapted from *Smile Therapy* by Liz Hodgkinson; pp. 108–9: *New Scientist* for adapted texts; p. 109: *The Times* for text adapted from 'August 14, 2116 – the End of the World?' by Nick Nuttal from *The Times* 26 October, 1992, © Times Newspapers Ltd. 1992.

**The authors and publishers are grateful to the following illustrators and photographic sources:**

**Illustrators:** Julie Anderson: pp. 51 *t*, 58, 71; Peter Byatt: pp. 13 *t*, 15, 17, 56, 66 *br*; Celia Chester: pp. 13 *b*, 92–3; Jerry Collins: pp. 55 *b*, 91 *b*, 118; Joanne Currie: p. 16 *t*; Richard Deverell: pp. 37, 94; Paul Dickinson: pp. 8, 65, 82–3; Lisa Hall: pp. 61 *b*, 66 *t*, 77 *b*; Sue Hillwood-Harris: p. 76; Phil Healey: pp. 74–5, 101; Frank Langford: pp. 16 *b*, 79; Angela Joliffe: pp. 64, 91 *t*; Vicky Lowe: pp. 66 *bl*, 78; Michael Ogden: pp. 11, 14, 88, 109 *t*; Amanda MacPhail: pp. 51 *b*, 55 *t*, 95, 117; Carl Melegari: p. 77 *t*; Nigel Paige: pp. 21, 84, 109 *b*; Bill Piggins: pp. 29, 42, 53, 61 *t*, 103 *t*, 113, 115, 119, 120; Tracy Rich: pp. 72, 103 *b*; Chris Ryley: p. 108; Jane Smith: pp. 23, 62; Sue Shields: p. 25; Kathy Ward: p. 98; Rosemary Woods: p. 43; Annabel Wright: pp. 10, 70, 81.

**Photographic sources:** Mohamed Ansar / Impact Photos: p. 90 *bl*; Apple Computer UK Ltd.: p. 36 *t*; Aqualisa for the focus spray from the Aqualisa Turbostream Power Shower System: p. 12 *bl*; Art Directors Photo Library: p. 24; Barnabys Picture Library: pp. 90 *br*, 117 *r*; The J. Allan Cash Photolibrary: pp. 90 *bc*, 117 *c*; Casio Electronics Ltd.: p. 36 *mc*; The Associated Press Ltd.: p. 65; Chinese and Japanese Special Fund, courtesy Museum of Fine Arts Boston for *Court Ladies Preparing Newly Woven Silk*: p. 34; Bruce Coleman Ltd.: pp. 107 *b*, 118; Colorific Photo Library: pp. 18, 73 *bl*, 117 *l*; Editions Minerva SA for pictures from *Life of the Aztecs in Ancient Mexico*, published by Productions Liber SA, 1978: p. 116; Mark Edwards / Still Pictures: p. 106 *m*; Greg Evans International: p. 68 *b*; Chris Fairclough Colour Library: p. 28 *bcr*; Mike Feeney / TRIP: p. 30; Sally and Richard Greenhill: pp. 31 *t*, 90 *ml*; Juliet Highet / TRIP: p. 90 *tl*; David Hoffman: p. 68 *tl*; The Hutchison Library: p. 106 *tl*; The Image Bank: p. 73 *br*; The Kobal Collection: p. 50; Peter Lake: pp. 12 *t*, *bc* & *br*, 20, 31 *b*, 39, 40–1, 44, 46, 54, 64, 81, 86 *br* (with thanks to Kate Dickens) & *bl*, 100, 104; Phil Loftus / Retna Pictures Ltd.: p. 66 *m*; Caroline Penn / Impact Photos: p. 90 *tcr*; Pictor International Ltd.: p. 86 *t*; Picturepoint-London: pp. 28 *bcl*, 66 *b*, 90 *mr*, 106 *tr*; Quadrant Picture Library: p. 52; Rex Features Ltd.: pp. 80, 106 *bl*; Helene Rogers / TRIP: pp. 31 *ml*, 86 *mr*; The Rolex Watch Company Ltd.: p. 86 *mcl*; Michael Rutland / Retna Pictures Ltd.: p. 86 *ml*; Sony United Kingdom Ltd.: p. 36 *mr*; South West News Service: p. 57; Tony Stone Images: pp. 9, 15, 28 *tl*, *bl* & *br*, 60, 73 *tl* & *m*, 106 *bc*, 107 *tl* & *tr*, 114, 120, 121; Sygma: p. 102; Syndication International: p. 66 *t*; Topham Picture Source: p. 86 *mcr*; Toshiba (UK) Ltd.: p. 36 *ml*; TROPIX / M. & V. Birley: p. 31 *mr*; TROPIX / M. Jory: p. 106 *tc*; Rob Turner / TRIP: p. 86 *bc*; Viewfinder Colour Photo Library: p. 29; Visionbank and England Scene: p. 68 *tr*; Zefa: pp. 28 *tr* & *m*, 73 *tr*, 90 *tcl* & *tr*, 107 *tc*, 112, 119.

*t* = top *m* = middle *b* = bottom *r* = right *c* = centre *l* = left

Picture research by Sandie Huskinson-Rolfe of PHOTOSEEKERS.